HOW TO WRITE & DESIGN A PROFESSIONAL RÉSUMÉ TO GET THE JOB

INSIDER SECRETS YOU NEED TO KNOW

With Companion CD-ROM

By Dale Mayer

How to Write & Design a Professional Résumé to Get the Job:
Insider Secrets You Need to Know – WITH COMPANION CD-ROM

Copyright © 2008 by Atlantic Publishing Group, Inc.
1405 SW 6th Ave. • Ocala, Florida 34471 • 800-814-1132 • 352-622-1875—Fax
Web site: www.atlantic-pub.com • E-mail: sales@atlantic-pub.com
SAN Number: 268-1250

ISBN-13: 978-1-60138-134-7   ISBN-10: 1-60138-134-4

Library of Congress Cataloging-in-Publication Data

Mayer, Dale, 1961-
  How to write and design a professional résumé to get the job : insider secrets you need to know : with companion CD-ROM / by Dale Mayer.
     p. cm.
  Includes bibliographical references and index.
  ISBN-13: 978-1-60138-134-7 (alk. paper)
  ISBN-10: 1-60138-134-4 (alk. paper)
  1. Résumés (Employment). I. Title.

  HF5383.M329 2008
  658.14'2--dc22
                          2008012242

Printed in the United States

Printed on Recycled Paper

We recently lost our beloved pet "Bear," who was not only our best and dearest friend but also the "Vice President of Sunshine" here at Atlantic Publishing. He did not receive a salary but worked tirelessly 24 hours a day to please his parents. Bear was a rescue dog that turned around and showered myself, my wife Sherri, his grandparents Jean, Bob, and Nancy and every person and animal he met (maybe not rabbits) with friendship and love. He made a lot of people smile every day.

We wanted you to know that a portion of the profits of this book will be donated to The Humane Society of the United States. *–Douglas & Sherri Brown*

The human-animal bond is as old as human history. We cherish our animal companions for their unconditional affection and acceptance. We feel a thrill when we glimpse wild creatures in their natural habitat or in our own backyard.

Unfortunately, the human-animal bond has at times been weakened. Humans have exploited some animal species to the point of extinction.

The Humane Society of the United States makes a difference in the lives of animals here at home and worldwide. The HSUS is dedicated to creating a world where our relationship with animals is guided by compassion. We seek a truly humane society in which animals are respected for their intrinsic value, and where the human-animal bond is strong.

Want to help animals? We have plenty of suggestions. Adopt a pet from a local shelter, join The Humane Society and be a part of our work to help companion animals and wildlife. You will be funding our educational, legislative, investigative, and outreach projects in the U.S. and across the globe.

Or perhaps you'd like to make a memorial donation in honor of a pet, friend, or relative? You can through our Kindred Spirits program. And if you'd like to contribute in a more structured way, our Planned Giving Office has suggestions about estate planning, annuities, and even gifts of stock that avoid capital gains taxes.

Maybe you have land that you would like to preserve as a lasting habitat for wildlife. Our Wildlife Land Trust can help you. Perhaps the land you want to share is a backyard— that's enough. Our Urban Wildlife Sanctuary Program will show you how to create a habitat for your wild neighbors.

So you see, it's easy to help animals. And The HSUS is here to help.

THE HUMANE SOCIETY
OF THE UNITED STATES.

2100 L Street NW • Washington, DC 20037 • 202-452-1100

www.hsus.org

TABLE OF CONTENTS

FOREWORD

In these tough economic times, companies are downsizing, outsourcing, merging, and job seekers are facing more competition than ever. You need a great résumé to stand out from the crowd. Your résumé should be a platform that details your achievements and experience. A résumé is a "marketing" document, designed to "sell" an employer on why they should contact and, ultimately, hire you.

As a Certified Professional Résumé Writer, I work everyday with individuals who, just like you, are looking for assistance with perfecting their résumés. In order to compete with other job seekers, your résumé must reflect not only your pertinent experience, but your professionalism as well. When embarking on a new career, you may possess all of necessary qualifications, but if they are not presented in a manner that correlates with the position you are applying for, your qualifications could be rendered insignificant.

How to Write and Design a Professional Résumé to Get the Job: Insider Secrets You Need to Know — With Companion CD-ROM is a complete guide to perfecting your complete résumé package. As someone who is committed to assisting clients with career change, I am impressed with the level of effort that author Dale Mayer has made to produce this book. She has performed a great deal of research in order to compile essential topics on writing professional résumés. She has reached out to leaders in our industry to obtain crucial information and insider secrets that will enable job seekers to land the job they want.

Mayer has organized the book in a way that is appealing to anyone wanting to design and create their own résumé. It covers everything from the basics of cover letters to the interview process. She has compiled a vast amount of information into a straightforward, easy-to-read book. This book is a great tool for job seekers who want more information on each step of the process, including today's job market, what to do after the interview, the power of words, and assessing yourself without being critical. With the CD-ROM, Mayer enables you to view various résumé styles that can be adapted to fit the different circumstances of each position in which you are applying for. Mayer has offered words of encouragement, great resources, and ideas for those unusual situations.

Career change can be an intimidating process, but with *How to Write and Design a Professional Résumé to Get the Job: Insider Secrets You Need to Know — With Companion CD-ROM* as a resource to help you along your journey, you are sure to come out on top. If you use all of this information, you will give yourself that edge over the competition that you deserve. Good luck in your job-seeking endeavors!

Camille Carboneau Roberts is a Career and Business Strategist who focuses on helping her clients get jobs! Her niche is helping people get jobs in the Federal government, transitioning Military to the corporate or Federal sectors, and helping government employees with promotions to the Senior Executive Service level. She creates marketing tools that get read! She started CC Computer Services & Training in 1989. In addition to this, her background includes working nine years for the prime contractor to the Department of Energy at the Idaho National Laboratory. She worked in a variety of positions including Electronic and Technical Publications, Human Resources, and Spent Fuel Processing. Camille has been awarded government contracts and managed 35 employees in a variety of services—electronic and technical word processing and editing services, résumé and career services, and engineering computer code calculations for nuclear research.

She has earned many credentials including:

Certified Federal Résumé Writer/Coach (CFRW/C)
Certified Professional Résumé Writer (CPRW)
Certified Employment Interview Professional (CEIP)
Certified Advanced Résumé Writer (CARW)
Certified Career Research Expert (CCRE)

Camille is active in several professional organizations including Career Directors International (Research Committee, Conference Committee), Professional Association of Résumé Writers & Career Coaches (Certification Committee), Career Masters Institute, and the Association of Online Résumé and Career Professionals.

Camille's work has been featured in 202 Great Résumés, 2500 Keywords to Get You Hired, 101 Best Résumés to Sell Yourself, Best Résumés for Grads, Best Résumés for College Students and New Grads, RésuméMaker Deluxe, Job Search Bloopers, *and* No-Nonsense Job Interviews: How to Impress Prospective Employers and Ace Any Interview.

Camille has also been nominated for three TORI Awards (Toast of the Résumé Industry) for Best International Résumé, Best Résumé for Job Re-Entry, and Best Cover Letter. She won the Idaho National Engineering and Environmental Laboratory Woman Owned Business Award and was recognized for being an Outstanding Supplier to the Idaho National Engineering and Environmental Laboratory. She may be contacted at Camille@ SuperiorResumes.com or through her website **www.SuperiorResumes.com**.

PREFACE

As a researcher, writer, and editor with many years of experience in the job-hunting wars, I wanted to write a comprehensive book that would help people understand not only what to do when it came time to write their résumés, but also why these things need to be done.

Today's job market is not the same as it once was. As young people come into the workforce more technologically knowledgeable than ever before, it seems that some of us are being caught up in a time warp, not knowing where we fit anymore. Indeed, we might wonder if we ever did fit. There are some wonderful jobs out there, some good jobs, and some jobs no one wants. When you find yourself in the midst of transition, whether you are in your mid-fifties and looking for only the second job in your life or you are in your mid-twenties and already looking for your tenth job, the problems are still the same — finding the right job for you.

That is harder than ever for those of us not born knowing what we wanted to do; the scope of careers available for consideration is huge. Too huge if you do not know yourself, your wants, likes and dislikes, and your skill set. For many, this is the place to start. It does not matter if you have spent forty years at a job you hate; today is a good day to start on a happier tomorrow. If that means a career change for only five more years, then let us make those five years good ones.

For those who have had changed forced on them, either through layoffs, a physical move as part of a family, or being fired, you have more control over your world than you think you do. Knowledge is power, and providing you with the knowledge you need is the purpose of this book. Arm yourself with the necessary tools of the trade, then head out and conquer your chosen path.

INTRODUCTION

Some people find it easy to dissect their lives and write up a résumé, while others would rather do anything than write about themselves. The trick to successfully writing a strong résumé is knowing what you like, what you want, what you can do, and what you have to offer. Therefore, it is important to spend some time understanding yourself, doing your research, learning the tools, and then making the time to write. Your résumé is not something that will likely happen overnight. It may be that you should not be the person writing it at all. If so, there are many excellent professionals out there to help you. However, if you think you are up to the challenge, then now is the time to get started.

This book is broken into different sections. The first covers the basics — helping those who need it try to figure out what you want for your next job. If you do not need this section, count yourself lucky and move on to the next. For those of you who need the worksheets, start at the beginning and answer the questions as honestly and succinctly as possible. There are no right or wrong answers, only good and better. Take your time, think about things, and come back to a question if you are having trouble. Work through the questions and then the summaries to get a clearer idea of what you want to do and what you might be good at. These worksheets are just to get you started. If you find they are not enough, consider going for assessment tests, particularly if you are at a crossroads in your life or are still trying to figure out what you are going to be when you grow up. Assessment can be done online or at various places in person. If this is the state of your life, these tests can help you sort out your next step.

Once you have completed the worksheets, you have the basics for moving on to understanding the fundamentals of a résumé. It is easy to copy someone else's or use a fill-in-the-blank template, but that is what it will look like you did. Take the time to understand what type of résumé is best for you and what should go into each section. Always collect your paperwork before starting so you can complete the first draft in one sitting. If you have to get up to go and find transcripts or check on dates, you interrupt the process and might have trouble getting back to it. Whenever possible, sit down and write the first draft at one time. Then take a break, think about the words you have down, and consider ways to strengthen your position by using words that are more powerful. Refer back to the book when you need to for suggestions and ideas. The book is intended as a resource for you to use to write the best résumé you can to get the job you want.

There are sections of the book that deal with special cases. No two people have the same history or the same problems. Read over the chapters that might pertain to your situation to see how to handle issues like a criminal record or having had only one employer. The solutions are there, and you need to understand how to apply them to your situation. It can be done, and quite successfully. The ability to create change is in your hands.

Once you have a professional-looking résumé, have one or two people proofread and edit it for you. They should, after less than a minute, understand the type of work you are looking for and the qualifications you can bring to the job. If they cannot, you need to rework the résumé. Be grateful for this critique because a recruiter will give your résumé much less than a minute of time to decide whether it has potential or goes in the garbage. Write your résumé, then proofread, edit, and rewrite if necessary. Do not let the résumé go out to any potential employer without taking the time to make it error-free. If your résumé shows that you do not care, neither will a recruiter.

Once you have a résumé that you are happy with, create other versions from this one. Make sure you have an electronic version to send out. It never hurts to have a PDF version to mail to an interested employer, and consider whether, in your industry and with your personality, you want to make a video or Web résumé. Neither eliminates the need for the fundamental paper version, but these other versions do show your technological skills and adaptability to change. Your résumé is representative of how you want yourself seen on a professional level.

Taking the time and the effort to write up a wonderful résumé will give you the potential for an interview. However, even a wonderful résumé is not going to get you a job if you do not have the right skills, cannot conduct yourself professionally in an interview, or if your references have nothing nice to say about you and your performance. The résumé is only part of the package required for getting the job you want. Learn about each piece of the package — do your best to make each piece shine like the professional you are, and you will get the job you deserve.

CHAPTER 1:

THE BASICS

There are certain situations in life that create major upheaval. Losing your job, facing the realization that you were in the wrong career, downsizing in your company, and enduring economic havoc are all events that can cause you to rethink your career path and question where you are going.

This process can be extremely difficult and stressful for you, your friends, and your family. Going through this period of exploration and uncertainty eventually leads to an understanding of the options available to you with the skills you have, potential areas of interest for retraining or additional training, and opportunities for a productive job search.

If you are ready for an employment change, looking for a new job can be exciting, as it will present you with a smorgasbord of possibilities.

This is a time of exploration, excitement, hope, fear, uncertainty, and confusion. The best way to handle this stressful time is to learn as much as you can, have the tools to deal with the issues, and to be prepared.

This is where this book comes in.

IF IT IS TIME FOR A CHANGE

There is a major difference between needing a career change and needing to change jobs. A career change is a huge, complex process. Some people have no doubts that it is time to walk a new path; others just want off their current path. The second group has an easier time choosing a new direction.

There are several good reasons to think about changing careers. Consider these points:

- **Your life has changed.** You might have been single when you set out on your career-driven path, working 12 to 14 hours a day, but now you are married with children on the way.

- **Your industry is undergoing radical change, and the outlook for your job does not look good.** The dot-com crash, for example, forced a career change on many people.

- **Your job is too stressful and may be affecting your health.** You may love your job, but the ulcer that has developed is making your life impossible. It is time for a less stressful job.

- **You are bored.** If you started down this path looking for something in particular, but only found monotony, it is time to change. This happens when you have advanced as far as you can in a company and there is nowhere else to go — except out.

- **A health condition requires you to change.** It is hard to imagine, but it does happen. If you were a veterinarian and developed animal hair allergies, or a heavy-equipment operator who can no longer sit for long hours because of a bad back, change would be mandatory.

There are many other scenarios in which people decide to make a career move. Making that decision, as hard as it can be, is nothing like deciding on what career to choose next.

If you decide that a career change is right for you — or if you are starting out and looking for your first career — the next step is to evaluate your skills, strengths, weaknesses, and values. There are many ways to do this. One choice is to seek the services of a career counselor or a career coach.

CAREER COUNSELORS AND COACHES

These professionals can help you understand and make choices for your career path. Whether you need to change careers, assess the one you are in, reenter the workforce, or deal with the many other workforce issues, these people are there to help.

Finding the right counselor can be a big challenge. Each of the following Web sites is a good source of information and suggestions, and some include full member lists for licensed professionals.

- **www.ncda.org** — At the National Career Development Association (NCDA), you will find information for consumers and job seekers, frequently asked questions, plus guidelines for selecting a career counselor.

- **www.nbcc.org** — The National Board for Certified Counselors focuses on credentialing counselors who meet the standards for general and specialty counseling practices. There is also a searchable database to help you find a counselor listed in the directory.

- **www.cce-global.org** — The Center for Credentialing & Education provides standards, training specifications, and credentialing for Career Development Facilitators.

- **www.counseling.org** — The American Counseling Association dedicates itself to the growth and development of the counseling profession.

- **www.coachfederation.org/ICF** — The International Coach Federation has a free Coach Referral Service that you can use to find a coach who matches your specific needs. The association has members located all over the globe.

- **www.acpinternational.org** — The Association of Career Professionals International has over 2,000 members in more than 30 countries.

Before you make a final choice, visit or phone the person. Make sure you are a good fit. There needs to be trust and understanding in this relationship to give you the best chance of making the right decisions.

To help you in your quest to sort out your career, these counselors may recommend or administer aptitude or assessment tests.

APTITUDE AND ASSESSMENT TESTS

Aptitude tests are tests that help you learn more about yourself. They can help you understand more about the things and conditions you like and those that you do not. This type of information will help you determine the best type of job for you. There are tests you can administer yourself, and tests that require interpretation assistance.

This assistance is provided by career counselors and other career professionals who specialize in these areas. You can do several free, self-administered, online tests, but others will cost $10 to $100.

These are tools, not tests, which have right or wrong answers. Each set of results requires a certain level of understanding, and although many new career suggestions will arise, they are only suggestions. It is up to you to understand and decide which career is suitable.

These tests are broken down into several categories:

- **Skills** — Here, the tests are designed to figure out what you are good at doing, what you like doing, and pointing out what skills you can add to your current skill set.

- **Values** — These assessments are designed to sort out what matters to you so you can find a good fit between your values and a job. These values include leisure time, flexible work schedule, high salaries, and even things like working indoors or outdoors.

- **Personality** — These tests look at your motivation, needs, attitudes, prejudices, and individual personality traits.

- **Interests** — These assessments are designed to highlight your likes and dislikes — the things you like to do, and the things you do not like to do. This type of test is based on the idea that people who have the same interests also enjoy the same types of jobs.

When looking at which tests to sign up for, consider the price — although it makes a difference to the pocketbook, it is not necessarily the best way to choose.

INTEREST TESTS

The goal with these tests is to find a match between a career and your interests. These are all fee-based at the time of writing.

- The Strong Interest Inventory at **www.cpp.com**

- The Career Key at **www.careerkey.org**

- Campbell Interest and Skill Survey (CISS) at **www. pearsonassessments.com**

SKILL TESTS

There are extensive types of these tests available online. Here are two free Web sites you can check out. Do an Internet search for many other options.

- Career One Stop at **www.careerinfonet.org**

- Career Intelligence at **www.career-intelligence.com**

VALUES INVENTORIES

These are tests to help you examine your personal values and motivations. The nature of these tests makes them personal and individualized.

- The Myers Briggs Personality Test is an assessment of different personality traits and values. You can purchase a variety of test options to fit your needs. Located at **www.myersbriggs.org.**

- Oscar, the occupation and skill computer-assisted researcher, has several tests available that can be found at **www.ioscar.org.**

After you have done these tests, look at the various suggestions the test results offer. It is time to explore these suggestions. The first thing to do is write down a list of occupations that show up repeatedly. Add to this list any jobs you are curious about but that did not show up on the test results. It is going to be an extensive list, and will need to be narrowed down.

The best way to narrow the choices down is to research the ones that have the highest appeal.

RESEARCHING JOBS

At this stage, your list should be no longer than ten jobs. For each of these jobs, you need to consider:

- The general job descriptions.

- The education requirements. Do you need to go back to school, and if so, is this something you are prepared to do?

- Whether you need to retrain or update existing skills.

- Whether this type of job will be around in ten years. Will you need to go through this career search process again?

- What type of advancement opportunities exist in this field – will this be enough for you?

- Whether the salary expectation is satisfactory — will you regret your decision in a couple of years when you cannot move your salary forward enough?

Here are three good resources to search for more information on various occupations:

- The U.S. Occupational Outlook Handbook, available at **http://www.bls.gov/oco/home.htm**

- Human Resources and Skills Development Canada has a similar database at **http://www23.hrdc-drhc.gc.ca/2001/e/generic/welcome.ehtml**

- About.com's career planning section has an occupation dictionary that can be found at **http://careerplanning.about.com/od/occupations/a/occ_dictionary.htm**

After this exploration process, you should have shortened the list down to a manageable few. If you are confident about your new job, you can move directly into the job search stage.

If you are not sure about one or two of the jobs on your list, informational interviews and even job shadowing are two steps you can take to help you gain a better understanding.

INFORMATIONAL INTERVIEW

An informational interview involves contacting several people who are currently working in the type of occupation you are considering. In this type of interview, done by phone, e-mail, or in person, you have a chance to ask these people questions about what they do, what they like, and what they do not like about the job. These interviews are between 15 and 30 minutes long.

JOB SHADOWING

Job shadowing involves going to the workplace of a person who is currently doing the occupation you are interested in doing. This way, you have a chance to observe the daily workload and responsibilities of the position. You can find out the typical hours in a workweek, the amount of overtime required, if any, the future job prospects, and even see where such a career might lead you. This type of information is valuable when making career choices.

At this point, you have narrowed your choices down to one field and several types of potential jobs in this one area. Your education fits the occupation and your skill level is in line, or else you are doing something about it. Now for the job search.

JOB SEARCH

Job searching today has never been easier; at the same time, it has never been harder. There are many job sites you can go to and check for every job available in your field and location. You can apply to several jobs at the same time with just a click of a button. The Internet is the best way to access the job market, but it can be a daunting process.

The problem many people face with an online job search is the sheer magnitude of the Internet. They tend to get bogged down as they travel from site to site. Confused and overwhelmed, many people post on general sites and leave it at that, hoping to attract the right attention. Learning to make good use of the many employment sites — general and niche sites — can help define your search and make it easier. It is worth the time and effort.

In Pam Dixon's book *Job Searching Online for Dummies*, she says, "17,000 new jobs are posted online each week and employers and recruiters use the Web to make 48 percent of all hires."

Of all the ways to find work online, general job sites are the most common. Some of the top sites for job hunters are:

- **Monster.com**

- **Careerbuilder.com**

- **Workopolis.com**

- **Hotjobs.yahoo.com**

- **Jobbankusa.com**

However, there are job search engine sites that will search job listings from thousands of Web sites, including job boards, newspapers, and the career pages of large companies. These types of search engines allow you to narrow down your search to company names, titles, and locations.

There are several of these sites. Here are a few:

- **Indeed.com**

- **SimplyHired.com**

- **Jobster.com**

It is important when researching to not exclude your local newspapers, as they often post their classified ads online. Also consider the popular **www. craigslist.com**.

Another choice is résumé banks, which allow you to post your résumé to an online database where recruiters and employers can access it. Often, these are online résumé forms where you have to fill out your employment history and skills. Other résumé banks allow you to cut and paste your entire résumé into the form. If you use the second format, make sure you create an electronic or ASCII résumé. See Chapter 4 for detailed information as to what is required for these types of résumés. An excellent resource can be found at the RileyGuide Web site: **www. rileyguide.com/multiple.html**. There you will find a full breakdown of each site and the URL.

After you find a job that looks interesting, take the time to learn more about the company. If everything looks good, you can tailor your résumé to that job.

During the job search process, do not forget the companies in your local area. Check out the various companies' Web sites. They will have a career page showing you the jobs available. Also, consider checking the local newspaper and phone directories.

It is important to check out every opportunity — you do not know which one will find you the job of a lifetime.

When you have found that job, it is time to write up your résumé.

WHAT IS A RÉSUMÉ?

There are many misconceptions as to what a résumé is. It is not a fictitious story line to pull the wool over the eyes of prospective employers, and it is not a biographical story.

A résumé is a communication tool that highlights what you can bring to the table. It shows what you have to offer a prospective employer.

Many people think that the process of sending out résumés is outdated. This same thinking is replacing résumés with interactive Web sites, blogs, video résumés, and online portfolios.

However, traditional résumés are still the standard for many industries. Times are changing, but they have not changed completely.

With that in mind, in the first part of this book, we are looking at what is traditional with résumés and later, we look at the trends of the future — trends that have already arrived for some people.

As résumés are the preferred method for applying for jobs, writing a résumé is where you need to start.

THE PURPOSE OF A RÉSUMÉ

The entire purpose behind a résumé is to display your talents so a prospective employer can see what you can bring to the company.

Your résumé has to market you in a short time. It needs to tell the recruiter or hiring manager immediately that you have what it takes. You have less than 30 seconds to either pass or fail this all-important first look.

The most effective way to do this is to address the employer's stated requirements for the position and then show the employer how you can meet them.

The problem with this is that people have trouble recognizing what is important enough to be included and what should not be considered in the first place.

A good résumé requires that you learn to be objective about your education, experience, skills, and accomplishments so you can find the hidden gems that show the prospective employer that you can give them the desired results.

To do this, you need to learn about the potential employer, the job, and yourself so that you can present your accomplishments in an easily accessible way.

WHAT MAKES A GREAT RÉSUMÉ?

A great résumé is a simple demonstration of your skills and abilities. It clearly shows what value you have to offer.

The rules to follow are simple:

1. Be clear and concise

2. Know the employer

3. Know yourself

4. Include only what is relevant to the position

5. Do not use three words if one will do

Keep it simple and only put down information you can back up. Do not lie on a résumé and do not fudge your dates. Recruiters and hiring managers do verify the information that you put down. Discrediting yourself is the fastest way to lose your dream job.

THE RIGHT LENGTH FOR YOUR RÉSUMÉ

Yesterday's advice on résumé length was to keep your résumé to one page. Today's advice is that a two-page résumé is fine. It is anybody's guess what advice will come tomorrow.

The best advice is to make your résumé the length that it needs to be to contain all the pertinent information as clearly and succinctly as possible. If that takes two pages, then it takes two pages.

Have other people read over your résumé and see what their impression is of your skills. Did they get the message you were trying to convey? However, each person who sees your résumé is going to have a different opinion, which might make things confusing.

That does not mean you should not show the finished document to anyone; on the contrary, show it to several people to get some valuable feedback. Listen to the comments, decide which ones make sense, and adapt your résumé appropriately. Do not listen to everyone, as some suggestions will be wrong. If the suggestions are not backed up with sound reasoning, they may be ignored.

THE MOST IMPORTANT THING TO REMEMBER

There is a lot to learn as you write your résumé, and the job can seem daunting as you work your way through the pages of this book.

The most important thing to remember about writing a résumé: Everything that goes on your résumé needs to be relevant to the job to which you are applying. If it is not pertinent, do not put it down. If it is personal, keep it personal and off the résumé.

THE BIGGEST MISTAKES OF ALL

Here is a list of some of the major mistakes repeatedly seen by recruiters and hiring managers:

1. **At the top of this list is lying.** This includes overinflating your skills and abilities. You should not make up jobs on your résumé, and you should not say you have skills that you do not have. Do not put down that you were a manager if you were an assistant. Do not say you are a pro at Excel if you only input some figures once or twice. These points will be checked, and your skills will fall short when you are on the job. The truth is the best answer.

2. **Not checking over and proofreading your résumé.** Do not send out a résumé full of spelling and grammar mistakes. Do not count on spell checkers to pick up errors. If you had wanted to put down form but typed from instead, the spell checkers do not know the difference. It is the same for was and saw. Both words are correctly spelled, depending on how they are used.

3. **Forgetting to include your contact information is the most common error.** It is particularly common on résumés submitted via the Internet.

4. **Inappropriate e-mail addresses.** Just because your friends know to use the e-mail address **iamstupid@hotmail.com** does not mean it is the e-mail address to put down on your résumé. If you do not have a generic address, it is time to make one.

5. **Résumé lacks focus to the job in question.** It is important to have your résumé focus on what skills and accomplishments you can bring to the company and job in question.

6. **Résumé is duty-driven and not accomplishment-driven.** Résumés should consist of high-impact, driven statements.

7. **Résumé buries the important skills instead of highlighting them.** This applies especially to computer skills, which should be displayed at the beginning.

CASE STUDY: SUSAN GUARNERI

Susan Guarneri, Certified Expert Résumé Writer and National Certified Career Counselor, is a 22-year veteran of the career counseling and career coaching industry. She started out as the Assistant to the Placement Director at The Johns Hopkins University (Baltimore). While there, she obtained her master's degree in Counseling and went on to specialize in career counseling. Her career has encompassed career development/outplacement work in the corporate, nonprofit, educational, government, and self-employment sectors.

She currently has a private practice in the beautiful Northwoods of Wisconsin, where she specializes in career assessments, career transition, personal branding, professional résumé writing, and online identity management for career development. Her Web sites are **www.assessmentgoddess.com** and **www.Resume-Magic.com.**

Susan has seen rapid change over the past two decades. Careers, career development, and job searching have become constantly changing dynamics that need maintenance, like exercising, to stay in shape. That is why she stresses the importance of ongoing career management, even after you land a job. Keeping networking fresh, résumés up to date, and branding at the top of your mind are all essential elements in proactively managing career growth. She sees us as already being in that "brave new world" of online career management driven by technology, including Web portfolios, online applications and résumé submittals, and mega-search engines for job hunting.

To make the most of your application in today's world, you must stand out in a relevant and positive way from your competitors. Show a personal branding value proposition that attracts attention, clearly lay out the proof to support your value, and make it easy to find in your application package.

There are important things you can do to maximize your résumé, and several things to avoid. She warns about the worst things people do on a résumé, such as the résumé having no focus, being boring, having errors and poor layout that hides the "golden nuggets," as well as offering no proof of relevant value to the employer.

CASE STUDY: SUSAN GUARNERI

To maximize your résumé, she suggests following these simple points:

1. **Focus** — what is your target career/job? "Generic" résumés and portfolios do not work.

2. **Relevancy** — build in relevant required and desired keywords, as well as relevant accomplishments

3. **Impact** — provide proof of your value via accomplishments

4. **Differentiation** — use your personal branding to stand out from your competitors

5. **Readability** — be concise and clear; leave enough white space and a large enough font for optimum readability

With her background, Susan has seen some of the major trends happening in today's job market. Changing careers and jobs is much more commonplace now; therefore, expect that it will happen to you and be vigilant in your career management efforts. Technology will continue to affect the world of careers—were there any blog editors ten years ago? Technology will also affect how employers and candidates find each other in the employability "dating game." The shift from job seeker to recruiter means that you must be visible and impressive online and with your network and industry in order to be found and "courted" as a passive candidate. Another trend Susan sees is an upward trend in self-employment, consulting gigs, flexible work schedules, job sharing, and telecommuting as Gen Y workers seek life/work balance.

Susan offers the following advice to today's job seekers:

"Two words: Courage and Commitment. Proactively go after the career and lifestyle of your dreams…then continue to monitor what works best for you as you and the world of work changes. Technology can work for you to uncover the ideal opportunities that fit you best. Do not wait to see a job posting online — your ideal job or career might never appear there. But that does not mean it does not exist."

CHAPTER 2:
KNOW THYSELF

To present the prospective employer with the best you have to offer, you have to know what you have to offer. That means getting to know yourself.

Over 2,000 years ago, Socrates said, "Know thyself." It is good advice, and it is called self-assessment. It is a good start to any job search or career change. Self-assessment is a process in which you learn more about your interests, strengths, and weaknesses, and even goals and values.

The benefits to this type of learning are many and include:

- Identifying strengths and weaknesses so you can emphasize or minimize certain factors

- Understanding your goals, both personal and career

- Seeing achievements and accomplishments that you may not have realized

- Building your confidence by pointing out the strengths and achievements you do have

- Bringing a sense of peace as you learn what you have and what you can do to learn more

This process, once started, seems endless. It will help you direct your life in a way that you would not have considered. You will be able to keep track of your strengths and skills, while identifying areas that could use improvement.

Self-assessment is great preparation for job interviews. You will be asked questions that are difficult to anticipate. Knowing the answer can make all the difference. These questions are along the lines of:

- What is your greatest weakness?

- What is your greatest strength?

- Describe your greatest accomplishment.

- Describe when you had to use your leadership skills last.

- What is your ideal job? Why?

- Where do you see yourself working in five years?

As you can see, these questions are intended to put you on the spot. Knowing and understanding your strengths and weaknesses makes it much easier to answer these questions. Start thinking now about potential questions so you are prepared for a job interview.

If you are unaware of what you want to do in life, or you are at a career crossroad, this time of minor self-assessment may not be enough. It is true that answers can come out of nowhere. However, you may want to consider career counseling and try some of the in-depth self-assessment tests that are available. You might be surprised at the answers and solutions.

This chapter will help you define your skills and accomplishments so that you can show the value you can add to a company. It is not hard, but it is a process. Work through the worksheets one section at a time.

SELF ASSESSMENT WORKSHEET

These are worksheets to help you understand yourself better. They are not meant to be conclusive, nor are they intended to replace the aptitude and assessment tests mentioned in Chapter 1. They are a place to start. For many people, this is all they need.

Rate on a scale of 1 to 5, with one being poor (or false) and five being excellent (or true):

SELF-ASSESSMENT

Part 1

Participation

_____ I like to listen to others share their ideas.

_____ I am happy to contribute my ideas.

_____ I like helping others in my group.

_____ I am an active group member.

_____ I like to share my expertise.

Learning

_____ I learn by doing.

_____ I learn by watching.

_____ I learn better from others.

_____ I learn quickly.

_____ I learn better on the job.

Skills

_____ I follow directions.

_____ I have enough skills to do what I want.

_____ I want to learn new skills.

_____ I plan on retraining.

_____ I want to learn an entire new skill set.

_____ I learned this new skill recently:_____

_____ I have improved in this skill:_____

Project Work

_____ I always do my best.

_____ I always do a good job.

_____ I enjoy seeing a project to the end.

_____ I like to work alone.

_____ I like to work on many projects at one time.

_____ I plan to learn more about _____.

Work Environment

_____ I like to work in close contact with others.

_____ I like to telecommute.

_____ I like to work in a large company.

_____ I contribute my ideas.

_____ I often ask others for their ideas and information.

_____ I always ask for help when I need it.

SELF-ASSESSMENT

_____ I always help other members of my group learn.

_____ I like to run the show.

_____ I help others keep on task.

_____ I always listen as much as I talk.

_____ I look others in the eye when speaking to them.

_____ I hate being singled out in a meeting.

_____ I like to run the meetings.

_____ I do not interrupt when others are speaking.

_____ I hate all meetings.

_____ I pull my weight in any job.

_____ I do not spread rumors and lies at work.

_____ I do an honest day's work.

_____ I respect others' feelings, even when I disagree with them.

_____ I want things my way.

_____ I praise others when appropriate.

_____ I always have to be right.

_____ I cooperate more than compete with others.

Write down all the items from the first list that warranted a 5. _____
_____

Write down all the items from the second list that warranted a 5. _____
_____

Any surprises? Did you think these would be the top items while you were doing this? Did you learn anything?

Now complete the following unfinished sentences:

    a) My two greatest strengths from the above list are:

        1. _____

        2. _____

    b) The two skills I have to work on from the above list are:

        1. _____

        2. _____

    c) My two greatest weaknesses are:

        1. _____

        2. _____

SELF-ASSESSMENT

d) I learned the following two new things about myself:

1. _____

2. _____

e) Two qualities I should work on are:

1. _____

2. _____

Some of the Ideas for these questions were adapted from Student Evaluation: A Teacher Handbook. (Appendix C: Sample Evaluation Forms)

WORKSHEET TO DETERMINE YOUR WORK VALUES

It is important to understand what you value in a work setting. These values are the set of standards that determine your attitudes, choices, and actions. Understanding your work values is an important foundation to planning your career moves. While one person might value salary, another might value prestige, and another might value location.

WORK VALUES WORKSHEET

From the list below, circle the ten values that are important in your next career choice. This is only a partial list, but it will make you think.

Flexibility	Challenge	Humor
Teamwork	Surroundings	Competition
Deadline pressure	Integrity	Achievement
Trust	Leading	Equality
Status	Cultural identity	Income
High earnings	Appreciation	Control
Prestige	Caring	Leading edge
Competence	Power	Creativity
Respect	Structure	Variety
Mastery	Influence	Independence

WORK VALUES WORKSHEET

Freedom	Risk	Predictability
Autonomy	Relaxed pace	Learning
Belonging	Harmony	Location
Detail-oriented	Appreciation	Work schedule

Now look at these ten and list the top five values in order of importance.

1. _____

2. _____

3. _____

4. _____

5. _____

From here, you can see what counts. Compare this list, in particular your top five choices, to your potential jobs. Ask yourself if they will give you the work environment you need at this time in your life.

LIFE AND WORK VALUES WORKSHEET

Look at the values listed below. Give each a number between 1 and 5, where five is extremely important and a 1 value is of low importance.

Work with people	Enjoy having day-to-day contact with people	
Work as part of a team	Working with a group toward common goals	
Make friends	Close personal relationships with coworkers	
Make decisions	The power to make decisions as part of your job	
Help society	Improve the world, people, and animals	
Help others	In some small or large way	
Work under pressure	Where time is short or work is judged by others	
Work alone	Do projects on your own	
Affiliation	Enjoy being a member of a particular group	
Intellectual status	Be regarded as an acknowledged expert	
Creativity	Create new ideas or programs	
Leadership	Be responsible for work done by others	

LIFE AND WORK VALUES WORKSHEET		
Variety	Work that changes often	
Routine	Job duties that are not likely to change	
Authority	Control the work activities of other people	
Influence people	Change attitudes or opinions of people	
Security	Being less threatened by changes in economy	
Fast pace	A high pace of activity; work is done rapidly	
Recognition	Be recognized for the quality of your work	
Excitement	A high degree of excitement in the job	
Profit/gain	Accumulating large amounts of money	
Independence	Work without significant direction from others	
Moral fulfillment	Contributing significantly to something	
Location	A place to live, which is tending to your life style	
Community	Getting involved in community affairs	
Challenge on a physical level	A job that makes physical demands you enjoy	
Technology	Using advances with technology	
Environmental concern	An organization that benefits the environment	
Not relocating	A job that allows a specific geographical area	
Advancement	Increases in work responsibilities and position	
Opportunities to learn	Opportunities to learn new things	
Time	You can work according to your own schedule	

As this is a partial list, here is an opportunity to write your own values and loose definitions: _____

_____

Now write down all the values that rated a 5 on your list above.: _____

_____

Now look at your Work Values Worksheet and compare it to the answers on the Life and Work Worksheets. Write down the top values from both worksheets. Do you see any similarities? Any comparisons or surprises? Try to list them in order of importance again. Have your priorities shifted? _____

_____

CASE STUDY: ANDREA KAY

Andrea Kay, career consultant, syndicated workplace columnist, and author of *Life's a Bitch and Then You Change Careers*, is also a sought-after speaker and executive coach. She has helped thousands of people take control of their lives and their careers. Since 1988, she has written a weekly column on careers and workplace issues that appears from California to New York to Canada, and globally, on the Web.

Andrea started in this industry by making her own career change in 1988 from writing promotional copy — which she loved doing, but always wondered what difference it made — to working as a freelance writer interviewing people on their careers. After evaluating her own skills, interests, and desires, she realized that this was her subject — her area where she could make a difference — and she built a career where she could write, speak, and counsel people in this industry.

Over the years, she has noticed more unhappy people with a desire for change who were at a point in their lives where they could make a change, or who understood that work was changing and they were going to have to adjust in order to stay valued.

Andrea still likes to focus on the fundamentals of résumés, noting that résumés have changed in presentation and the industry has changed in that it is catering to an electronic industry; however, the fundamental content is still the same. When a company is hiring you, they are looking for a problem solver. Your cover letter is where you address the particular problem. It is important to know what the problem is, how you can solve it, and what examples in your history you have to prove it.

Focus your résumé on problem solving and demonstrate these abilities; make the information relevant to the role, the position, and how you want people to see you; show your characteristics and personality and let the recruiter see who you are. Keep your résumé simple, easy to read, and professional.

Andrea says not to let your fears drive the process. People become afraid of what is happening, or afraid that nothing will happen. They become paralyzed and make decisions based on these fears. Decide who you are and what your brand is — do not get bogged down by fear.

Decide what you want to say about yourself, and how you want others to see you. Then learn how to put out that consistent message in the way you dress, talk, and interact. The rest will follow.

CHAPTER 3:

TRADITIONAL RÉSUMÉ STYLES

There is no shortage of advice available to job seekers. Today's job hunters are inundated with suggestions and tips on how to describe their backgrounds, skills, and achievements. There are more formats and templates, looks, and designs to confuse the issue even further. Of these, a couple of basic formats suit most people's needs. Each has pros and cons. Your choice will depend on the circumstances of your potential job.

Take the time to review each of the different formats. Read about the variations and check out the examples so you can make an informed decision. The goal is to be noticed by the HR specialists and recruiters. You want your résumé to be one of the 10 percent picked for consideration.

The goal of any résumé is to win a job interview.

CHRONOLOGICAL

A chronological résumé is one that follows a sequence of one thing after another based on time. All your work experience is listed in reverse chronological order, with your current or most recent job first. This is often the preferred method for recruiters, hiring managers, and HR specialists because it is easy to read and quickly shows your progressive work experience and growth. These people do not have and will not take the time to sort through information to find what they need to know. You have to make it easy for them.

For anyone with a solid, logical work history, this style is a good choice. However, it is a poor style choice if your last position is not related to the job you are applying for.

There are three basic elements of a chronological résumé:

1. There is an introduction or summary of your key strengths and qualifications. The heading for this section can be called any of the following: Profile, Professional Summary, Career Summary, or Summary of Qualifications.

2. The second element is your work experience. This section needs to include the name of your current or your most recent employer, followed by the city and state of where the company is located, and then the dates of your employment. There should be job titles and a brief summary of your accomplishments.

3. The third major element is the accomplishments sections. This is the most critical section of any résumé. List each according to the position and add their relevance to the job you are applying for. It is important to discuss anything new you brought in or any innovation you played a part in; these accomplishments are highly regarded. Put accomplishments in context so the reader can understand how your accomplishments fit in to the whole scope of the industry. If you say that, during your stint in the marketing department, sales increased by 10 percent, you need to state that it is because of your proposal; otherwise, the company sales as a whole could have increased because of general economics and not your contribution. Using facts and figures adds punch and clarity.

Use this format when:

1. You have a stable and steady work history.

2. You continued to work mostly in one industry or job type.

3. You are applying for a job in the same field as your work history.

4. You are looking for a similar or more senior job in the same industry.

5. Your most recent position is the one most likely to impress — because

this job will be at the top of the page in this résumé format, it needs to be a good one and relevant to the position for which you are applying.

Tips for this type of format:

- List the jobs that are the closest to the one you are applying for.

- Keep the list relatively short.

- List your most recent job first.

The disadvantages of this type of format:

- It highlights employment gaps.

- It could show an unstable work history.

- It does not highlight skills as much as work history.

SAMPLE CHRONOLOGICAL RÉSUMÉ (ONLY ONE OF MANY OPTIONS)

Name
Street Address
City, State ZIP
Telephone Number
E-mail Address

Objective (optional)
- This is one or two sentences describing your employment goals
- What you want to do

PROFESSIONAL SUMMARY (optional)
- Number of years experience in relevant paid or unpaid work
- Highlight the experience relevant to the job
- Three to five sentences long
- Emphasize results
- Relevant accomplishment/skill/attribute
- Related special knowledge, training, or certification

EXPERIENCE
Job Title, City
(Month/Year - Month/Year)
- Brief overview of duties in bullet form
- Explain your accomplishments

SAMPLE CHRONOLOGICAL RÉSUMÉ (ONLY ONE OF MANY OPTIONS)

- Focus on the actions or end result; the solutions you found to problems
- Do not just list responsibilities or duties
- Tell what solutions you found, changes you implemented, and what the results were
- Include industry terms
- List facts and figures
- Start with action words and do not reuse words, if possible
- The most recent job gets the most attention on your résumé

Previous Job Title, City
(Month/Year - Month/Year)

- The information on the second job is a little shorter
- Keep information relevant to the position
- Use keywords and keep it short
- You have 15 seconds to make the recruiter's cut
- Focus on the results that you created
- Do not list your job description because this only says what you were expected to do

Earlier Job Title, City
(Month/Year – Month/Year)

- Put down fewer points for this job
- That means the information has to be the most important to make it onto the résumé

EDUCATION
Degree, University, City

- GPA (only if higher than 3.5)
- Honors received
- Pertinent recognition or other information

Next Degree

- List any other degree(s) as per above
- Keep the information pertinent to the job

SKILLS/QUALIFICATIONS

- List your skills that relate directly to the position or career field that you are applying for; i.e., computer skills
- If you are in a technology field, it is suggested that this section appear at the top under professional summary
- If posting your résumé online, this is a good place to include relevant keywords

MEMBERSHIPS/AFFILIATIONS (optional)

- Professional memberships and volunteer work show your commitment to your industry and community. Mention leadership positions and briefly note relevant achievements.

SAMPLE CHRONOLOGICAL RÉSUMÉ (ONLY ONE OF MANY OPTIONS)

- This is especially valuable for recent graduates and career changers to demonstrate that you are making an effort to establish yourself in a new field.

FUNCTIONAL

A functional résumé focuses on your skills and experience, rather than on your recent work history. This format highlights talents and accomplishments so managers and recruiters can quickly and easily spot what they are looking for. At the same time, it minimizes anything negative that a chronological format would highlight, which makes it a good choice for people who are changing careers or who have gaps in their employment history.

There are three basic elements of this format:

1   As in the chronological résumé, the functional résumé format starts with an introduction or summary of your key strengths and qualifications. The heading for this section can be called any of the following: Profile, Summary, Career Summary, or Summary of Qualifications.

2   The second element is where you discuss your successes. Here, try to create three to five different areas to highlight. Suggestions can be from any area, such as New Research Development, Advertising and Sales Promotions, General Management, or even Recruitment. Whatever specialized areas you are experienced in, create a list of your accomplishments.

3   The third element in this résumé format is your employment history. As before, you list the employers, their locations, and the dates when you worked for them. There is some discussion again as to the benefit of listing your job title. An easy rule to follow is decide whether the job title is relevant to the new position; if so, include it.

Think carefully about using this type of résumé. It could backfire on you. It is not the preferred format, and many recruiters are unfamiliar with it. It does highlight your key strengths and achievements; however, the reader has to search for when and where these accomplishments occurred.

Use this format when:

1. You are considering a change of careers.

2. You are considering returning to a previous career field.

3. There are gaps in your work history.

4. There are achievements that are outside work, such as hobbies, sports, or volunteer work.

5. You have recently graduated from high school or college.

6. You have been out of the job market for some time (an example is a homemaker returning to work).

Tips for writing this type of résumé:

- Focus on your work skills and accomplishments.

- Focus on your transferable skills. These are skills you have learned in one field that can be transferred to other fields.

- Do not list what does not relate to your job goal.

Disadvantages of using this format:

- Your experience is directed to specific jobs and dates of employment—recruiters may suspect that you are hiding something.

- It does not highlight career growth.

Recruiters have a hard time seeing what the applicant did in the various jobs.

SAMPLE FUNCTIONAL RÉSUMÉ (SIMPLE VERSION))

Name
Street Address
City, State ZIP
Telephone Number
E-mail Address

Objective (optional)
- This is one or two sentences describing your employment goals
- What you want to do

PROFESSIONAL SUMMARY (optional)
- Number of years of experience in relevant paid or unpaid work
- Highlight the experience relevant to the job
- Three to five sentences long
- Emphasize results
- Relevant accomplishment/skill/attribute
- Related special knowledge, training, or certification

Education (if related to job)
Candidate for (unless already graduated) Degree Name, Specialization, Institution, City, Date Begun – present (or year of graduation)
- Relevant Courses: Three to six related to objective listed by course name
- Relevant Project
- Thesis
- Awards (if not creating separate section)

Other education, including certificates. Only list high school if you are in the first year of postsecondary studies.

Experience or Skill
- Accomplishments relevant to job objective, preferably detailing unique actions and benefits, beginning with action verbs, taken from paid or unpaid work, or academic or life experience

EXAMPLE TWO OF FUNCTIONAL RESUME

NAME
Address
City, State ZIP
Telephone Number
E-mail Address

PROFILE
OBJECTIVE
AREAS OF EXPERTISE (these are suggestions)
- Management expertise
- Customer relations

EXAMPLE TWO OF FUNCTIONAL RESUME

- Administration
- Accounting/Budgeting

EMPLOYMENT

COMPANY NAME, City, State   Start and end date
Job Title
Accomplishments
COMPANY NAME, City, State   Start and end date
Job Title
Accomplishments
COMPANY NAME, City, State   Start and end date
Job Title

Accomplishments

FUNCTIONAL SKILLS

-
-

PERSONAL SKILLS

-
-

EDUCATION

INSTITUTION NAME, City, State
Start and end date
Degree, Diploma, Certificate/Specialization, Majors
INSTITUTION NAME, City, State
Start and end date
Degree, Diploma, Certificate/Specialization, Majors

ACADEMIC ACHIEVEMENTS

Name of awards, scholarships

-
-

PROFESSIONAL DEVELOPMENT

-
-

MEMBERSHIPS/ASSOCIATIONS

ASSOCIATION NAME and location   Start and end date
Membership Title (month/year)
Next Association   Start and end date

VOLUNTEER EXPERIENCE

- NAME OF ORGANIZATION, City, State   Start and end date
  Job Title or Area Worked (month/year)

EXAMPLE TWO OF FUNCTIONAL RESUME

- Next experience

INTERESTS

References will be made available during the interview

COMBINATION OR HYBRID RÉSUMÉ FORMAT

This type of format is an attempt to address the problems of a functional résumé format by explaining where and when the successes you listed occurred. In other words, it combines several features of the first two formats to create a hybrid.

You can highlight your skills in this format, and you can provide the chronological work history that the managers and recruiters are looking for.

Use this format when you want to:

1. Emphasize unique skills and accomplishments.

2. Lessen the importance of your employment history.

Tips for writing this type of résumé:

- Divide your experience into several areas to show what you have accomplished. This is the same as a functional résumé.

- List your employers, job titles, and work years — keep this section short.

Disadvantages of this format:

- The résumé can be long and tedious to go through.

- The résumé could have repeated information.

Here is a sample combination of a hybrid résumé format. There are many styles, designs, and sections that you can have. What matters is that what goes down is pertinent to your objective and the job for which you are applying.

SAMPLE COMBINATION OR HYBRID RÉSUMÉ

	Your Full Address	Phone Number
	City, State, ZIP Code	E-mail Address

Your Name

Objective	Put objective here
Career Highlights	• List just the highlights
	• Focus on accomplishments
	• Use facts and figures when possible
	• List strong skills that are pertinent to position
	• List data management and computer skills

Educational Background	Start and end date School/Organization name
	Diploma/Certificate/Major City/State
	• Details of education completed
	• Next education level

Employment History	Start and end date Company/Organization name
	Job title City, State
	Details of position
	Start and end date Company/Organization name
	Job title City, State
	Details of position

Relevant Courses/Training	List those relevant to position
Related Skills	List those relevant to position
Awards	List all major awards
Languages	List all languages that you speak/write
Interests and Activities	List hobbies, sports, and interests

TARGETED

A targeted résumé is one customized to highlight experiences that are relevant to the job for which you are applying. It takes more time and effort to write a targeted résumé, but it is worth it. The stakes are high when a perfect job comes along that seems just right for your qualifications and experience — so take the time to get it right and you will be more likely to get the job.

One of the easiest ways to target your résumé, instead of rewriting it, is to include a Career Highlights section or, as it is also called — a Summary of Qualifications. This goes at the top of your résumés; it is the first thing a recruiter or manager will see. After this section, you carry on with your list of work experiences in chronological order, just as in a traditional résumé.

In the previous formats, the Career Summary or Professional Summary was optional. With a targeted résumé, it is mandatory.

When you write a targeted résumé, make sure you carry the same theme forward and write up a targeted cover letter.

SAMPLE TARGETED RÉSUMÉ

Name
Street Address
City, State ZIP
Phone Number
E-mail Address

Objective: Here you say that you are applying for a certain type of job

Relevant Skills and Experience
- Show how your skills meet the job requirements
- List three to five points
- Focus on accomplishments
- Show the results of what you accomplished

Work History – only include jobs that are directly relevant to position or objective

COMPANY NAME, City, State	Start and end date

Job Title
Accomplishments

COMPANY NAME, City, State	Start and end date

Job Title
Accomplishments

COMPANY NAME, City, State	Start and end date

Job Title
Accomplishments

Education — List the education relevant to position

INSTITUTION NAME, City, State	Start and end date

Degree, Diploma, Certificate/Specialization, Majors

INSTITUTION NAME, City, State	Start and end date

Degree, Diploma, Certificate/Specialization, Majors

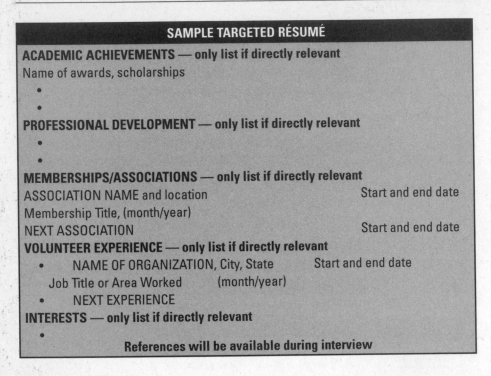

SAMPLE TARGETED RÉSUMÉ

ACADEMIC ACHIEVEMENTS — only list if directly relevant
Name of awards, scholarships
-
-

PROFESSIONAL DEVELOPMENT — only list if directly relevant
-
-

MEMBERSHIPS/ASSOCIATIONS — only list if directly relevant
ASSOCIATION NAME and location   Start and end date
Membership Title, (month/year)
NEXT ASSOCIATION   Start and end date
VOLUNTEER EXPERIENCE — only list if directly relevant
- NAME OF ORGANIZATION, City, State   Start and end date
  Job Title or Area Worked   (month/year)
- NEXT EXPERIENCE
INTERESTS — only list if directly relevant
-
                References will be available during interview

CREATIVE

This type of résumé is where you get to unleash your creativity to the point where almost anything goes — almost. You need to include the required information; however, you get to package it in a fun way. This type of résumé format works if you are applying for a position in advertising or the arts. In these positions, creativity is a strong requirement for the job. These résumés are not for everyone.

A creative résumé is also not scannable, which means, after being submitted to a company, the résumé cannot be scanned into their database. Think about where you are sending your résumé — what is the chance that a gallery or ad agency is going to ask for a scannable résumé? If you decide you need to, send two résumés — one in ASCII text format and your creative résumé.

Keep readability in mind as you create this résumé. If the hiring manager cannot read the information easily, you will not be called for a job interview.

SAMPLE CREATIVE RÉSUMÉ

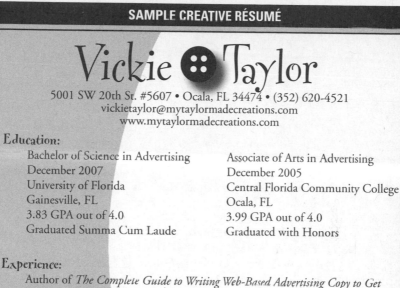

Vickie Taylor

5001 SW 20th St. #5607 • Ocala, FL 34474 • (352) 620-4521
vickietaylor@mytaylormadecreations.com
www.mytaylormadecreations.com

Education:

Bachelor of Science in Advertising
December 2007
University of Florida
Gainesville, FL
3.83 GPA out of 4.0
Graduated Summa Cum Laude

Associate of Arts in Advertising
December 2005
Central Florida Community College
Ocala, FL
3.99 GPA out of 4.0
Graduated with Honors

Experience:

Author of *The Complete Guide to Writing Web-Based Advertising Copy to Get the Sale*, Published 2008

Graphic Designer, Atlantic Publishing Company, May 2007 — Present, Ocala, FL
* Responsible for laying out an average of 2 books per week
* Designed book covers, advertisements, and interior layouts
* Proofread books for final printing
* Worked with two printers to ensure quality book printing

Art Director, Airboat World Magazine, August 2004 — August 2006, Ocala, FL
* Designed over 100 advertisements for 50 different advertisers
* Monthly magazine had over 10,000 copies distributed internationally
* Developed promotional fliers, inserts, cozies, hats, and T-shirts
* Managed a three person staff to create effective advertisements and designs

Art Director, Southern 4x4 Magazine, March 2006 — August 2006, Ocala, FL
* Created design for layouts, advertisements, logos, and graphics of initial publication of a bi-monthly magazine

Freelance Designer, August 2005 — Present, Ocala, FL
* Designed advertisements and logos for multiple businesses and people
* Managed time and finances for business

SAMPLE CREATIVE RÉSUMÉ

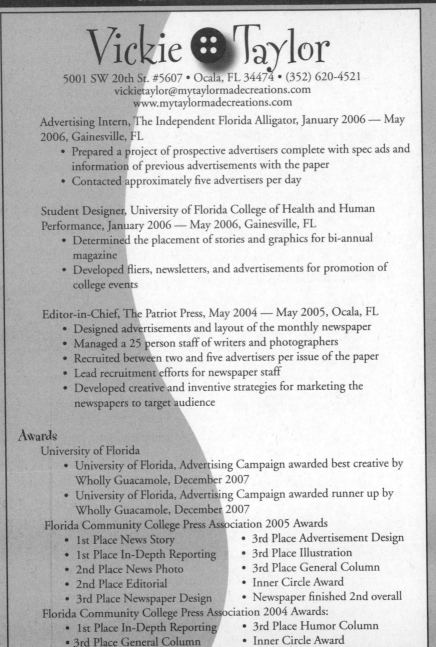

Vickie ⬤ Taylor

5001 SW 20th St. #5607 • Ocala, FL 34474 • (352) 620-4521
vickietaylor@mytaylormadecreations.com
www.mytaylormadecreations.com

Advertising Intern, The Independent Florida Alligator, January 2006 — May 2006, Gainesville, FL
- Prepared a project of prospective advertisers complete with spec ads and information of previous advertisements with the paper
- Contacted approximately five advertisers per day

Student Designer, University of Florida College of Health and Human Performance, January 2006 — May 2006, Gainesville, FL
- Determined the placement of stories and graphics for bi-annual magazine
- Developed fliers, newsletters, and advertisements for promotion of college events

Editor-in-Chief, The Patriot Press, May 2004 — May 2005, Ocala, FL
- Designed advertisements and layout of the monthly newspaper
- Managed a 25 person staff of writers and photographers
- Recruited between two and five advertisers per issue of the paper
- Lead recruitment efforts for newspaper staff
- Developed creative and inventive strategies for marketing the newspapers to target audience

Awards
University of Florida
- University of Florida, Advertising Campaign awarded best creative by Wholly Guacamole, December 2007
- University of Florida, Advertising Campaign awarded runner up by Wholly Guacamole, December 2007

Florida Community College Press Association 2005 Awards
- 1st Place News Story
- 1st Place In-Depth Reporting
- 2nd Place News Photo
- 2nd Place Editorial
- 3rd Place Newspaper Design
- 3rd Place Advertisement Design
- 3rd Place Illustration
- 3rd Place General Column
- Inner Circle Award
- Newspaper finished 2nd overall

Florida Community College Press Association 2004 Awards:
- 1st Place In-Depth Reporting
- 3rd Place General Column
- 3rd Place Humor Column
- Inner Circle Award

Often with a creative résumé, a portfolio is required. This portfolio is at least as important as the résumé, if not more important, and is covered in detail in Chapter 14.

The previous résumé is that of a graphic designer with a degree and background in advertising. It has some of the standard résumé formats, with a more creative touch. It is a visually attractive résumé, with excellent use of colors to highlight aspects of the résumé like name, areas of experience, and Web addresses (see the full color version on the companion CD-ROM). The eye-catching style plays up the impact of alignment, spacing, and color. The length is appropriate.

Some more extreme creative résumés will have pictures as the background or watermarks set behind the text, making them look more like posters, but in the standard paper size. Other creative résumés may look more like scrapbook pages that have small embellishments added to be considered unique and attention-grabbing. These are all appropriate, depending on the industry you are in and the type of work you are applying for.

CURRICULUM VITAE

The term curriculum vitae (CV) means "course of one's life." This document is a detailed overview of the academic and professional course of your life. It is longer and more detailed than a résumé and tends to be for educators and scientists. Résumés are more commonly used for business and industry. CVs are the preferred form for the following types of positions:

- Admission to graduate school (can be part of an application for a graduate scholarship)

- Grant proposals

- Teaching and higher-level administrative positions in college and university

- Academic and tenure reviews

- Speaking engagements

- Publishing review boards

- School administration positions — superintendent, principal, or department head level

- Research and consulting positions

CVs are longer than résumés. Résumés are one to two pages at the most, whereas curricula vitae are two pages minimum. For a bachelor's or master's degree candidate, two to three pages is common, two to five for a doctoral candidate, and five or more pages is common for an experienced researcher.

It is important to write this document in a clean, easy-to-read style. The document needs to include your professional publications, presentations, committee work, grants received, and any other pertinent information. Include everything from the following list that pertains to you and the position you are applying for:

- Education — including master's thesis, dissertation topic, areas of concentration of graduate study, academic awards, scholarships and fellowships, certificates and licensure, and special training

- Teaching experience

- Research experience

- Consulting experience

- Publications

- Professional papers and presentations

- Grants received

- Professional associations

- Professional papers and presentations

- Language competencies

- Foreign study and travel abroad

Even though CVs are preferred for some disciplines, the format and content can vary from one discipline to another. You need to find the standard format and content for your area of expertise.

The following is an outline of a CV, showing what belongs on it.

SAMPLE CURRICULUM VITAE

Your Contact Information
Name
Address
Telephone
Cell Phone
E-mail

Personal Information
Date of Birth
Place of Birth
Citizenship
Visa Status
Gender

Optional Personal Information
Marital Status
Spouse's Name
Children

Employment History
List each employer separately, but only go back ten to fifteen years.
Work History
Academic Positions
Research and Training

Education — Can list most recent education first
Include dates, majors, training, and certification
High School
University

SAMPLE CURRICULUM VITAE

Graduate School
Postdoctoral Training

Professional Qualifications
Certifications
Accreditations
Computer Skills

Awards
Put down any major awards received

Publications
List your published works; include the title, the date, where it was published, by whom, and in what issue

Books
List your published books here and be sure to include full details, just as for the other publications.

Professional Memberships
List here all the professional groups to which you belong. List the full names if the acronyms are not clear. Give brief descriptions of the type of association.

Interests
Include interests, like hobbies and sports.

CASE STUDY: SUSANN CAMUS

Susann Camus is a nationally certified human resources professional with more than ten years of consulting experience in organizational communications, training, employee relations, compensation, succession planning, and recruitment and retention. She has managed human resources for private organizations and consulted with job hunters and small, medium, and large public and private organizations. Susann can be reached through her consulting practice at **certcomm@mac.com**

Susann was working in a communications role when the president of her organization announced an intensive continuous quality improvement initiative and asked for volunteers. She was one of six employees from a pool of 1,000 to be selected and given intensive training. Working alongside professional trainers was exciting, and she ended up drawing on her communication and training skills to enter the HR field full time. Subsequently, she studied HR in continuing education programs.

CASE STUDY: SUSANN CAMUS

According to Susann, the changes over the last decade have shown more:

1) Embracing of technology in terms of using human resource information systems to manage employee data; use of information systems to accept, evaluate, and store online job applications.

2) Emphasis on competency-based human resources, with increased recognition of the importance of individuals who are technically literate and have highly developed "soft" skills (e.g., interpersonal skills, team skills, listening skills, speaking and writing skills, problem-solving abilities, flexibility and adaptability, and openness to change).

For the future, job hunters need to demonstrate computer literacy (e.g., mastery of e-mail, Internet search engines, word processing, and presentation and spreadsheet software), mastery of the knowledge and skills specific to their discipline, and highly developed soft-skill competencies.

Job seekers also need to use the format requested by the prospective employer and verify that the information provided closely corresponds to the needs expressed in the job posting. Susann warns against lying, providing too much information — particularly personal, irrelevant work information — as well as supplying references without having first contacted them to request their permission.

Susann recommends tailoring the résumé and portfolio to the job and using keywords so that an automated, computer-based recruitment system will highlight your application as having a high number of matches with the ad, and therefore, deserving of more attention. List job-related, measurable accomplishments and highlights (e.g., improved customer satisfaction by 85 percent, reduced processing time from two months to 48 hours, completed the project on time and under budget) at the top of the body of your résumé. In addition, she suggests having someone else proofread your résumé and portfolio so it is error free. Always respect submission guidelines by submitting applications by the deadline and in the preferred format.

As for design elements, Susann adds, "Since a recruiter spends about 20 seconds skimming a résumé, you want a design that encourages the recruiter to read highlights. Keep the design simple, yet elegant. Use color sparingly to highlight headings that denote different sections, but make sure the color is dark enough to read when the document is printed using a black-and-white printer. Use bullets for body text. Be consistent with typefaces (e.g., serif typeface for headings, sans-serif for body text) and formatting."

Employers are looking for candidates who are competent in their field, are technologically perceptive (know word-processing, presentation, and spreadsheet

CASE STUDY: SUSANN CAMUS

software and how to use search engines; knowledge of database applications is a huge asset), flexible, and can adapt to changing organizational priorities and a changing work environment.

Her advice for today's job seeker is very comprehensive because she has seen the best and the worst of the current job market. She suggests:

1. Do your homework before preparing your cover letter, application, and portfolio. Research the organization you wish to work for by browsing their Web site, scanning their annual report, identifying the HR manager or recruiter by name and title, and searching for recent media coverage on the organization/industry.

2. If you know someone in the organization, contact them and ask if you can mention their name in your application. Or, if you know someone in the same industry in a different organization, ask that person for the name of a contact in the organization to which you are applying. Prior to preparing the application, get in touch with this contact and ask whether you can refer to them in your cover letter. Experience and expertise are crucial, but connections count, and are a good way to get your foot in the door.

3. Target your cover letter and résumé to fit the job and the organization. In your cover letter and résumé, use key words from the posting to increase your chances of being selected for an interview. Emphasize how your competencies fit with, and can benefit, the organization.

4. Contact your references prior to going to an interview.

5. Adjust clothing and check teeth and hair prior to entering the reception area. Arrive five to ten minutes early and present a relaxed appearance in the waiting room. Greet the receptionist in a pleasant manner. Do not fidget; do not listen to your iPod while waiting.

6. When the recruiter comes out to greet you, stand up, make eye contact, shake hands confidently, and introduce yourself with a friendly smile, making a winning first impression.

7. Minimize the risk of making a mess by courteously declining any offer of coffee or water.

8. Ask questions to demonstrate your proactive approach to work.

9. Send thank-you notes to both the HR recruiter and the work manager following the interview. Send the thank yous electronically within 24 hours of the interview or via a handwritten thank-you card within 48 hours of the interview. Doing either

CASE STUDY: SUSANN CAMUS

will make you stand out, since only 25 percent of job applicants send thank-you notes.

10. If you remember something crucial after the interview has ended, send a follow-up note, prefacing it with: "In addition to my skills in..., I thought you might find it useful to know that when I worked at..., I took on additional responsibilities in the area of.... We were successful...."

11. Follow up with a very polite phone call or e-mail if you have not heard from the recruiter within two weeks of your interview.

12. If you are told you are not the successful candidate for a position, ask the recruiter whether they have any recommendation as to how you can strengthen your prospects for success as you continue your job hunt. Appeal to the recruiter as an expert, and do not argue with any assessment offered. Thank the recruiter and move on.

13. If you are offered a position, provide at least two weeks' notice to your current employer so she or he can plan for your replacement. This will show prospective employers that you are a professional and care about your work footprint.

CHAPTER 4:
NEW TECHNOLOGY RÉSUMÉ STYLES

The Internet era has brought change to the job-hunting world. Decades ago, job hunting required hours of legwork and hard labor. There were newspapers to scour looking for potential jobs, cover letters and résumés to type and mail, and hours of waiting required.

Some of those things are similar today — we still spend hours scouring the Internet, looking at job sites and company Web sites for employment opportunities. We read classified ads online and, of course, we send our résumés via e-mail, online application forms, mail, and fax.

What happens to our résumé, though, when we mail or fax it to companies that are going to scan the résumé into their computerized database?

When it is received by the human resources department, it is reviewed by the recruiter and put into a pile for that job posting. Your résumé is transferred from paper to a digital database with a special scanner system called Optical Character Recognition, or OCR. The scanner passes over the piece of paper and begins interpreting and filling in the form to create your electronic résumé.

This OCR system recognizes patterns on the printed page by the dots of ink in each letter. It matches these patterns with characters in its memory. As they do not hold all available fonts in its memory, you need to use standard fonts for proper recognition. If the machine cannot recognize your font, the letters will be misinterpreted and your words will not be spelled correctly.

The purpose of using this type of software is so the recruiter can type in a keyword search and pull up all résumés that contain that word. Yours will not be included if the computer could not translate your font correctly. Misspelled words will not be picked up by the search engine.

This is why it is important to make some design changes specifically for scanning to keep your résumé a viable marketing tool.

When looking at the application requirements for a company, see if a scannable résumé is required before sending yours.

Let us look at the different types of electronic résumés.

SCANNABLE

In some cases, it is necessary to convert your résumé into a scannable format. This allows the résumé to be optically scanned and placed into a computer database where employers can review it. It is becoming a more common requirement. It is also to your advantage to follow these simple rules in order for the finer points of your résumé to be translated into the database correctly.

The term "scannable" is often used interchangeably with the term "electronic format." However, there are slight differences.

Here are some tips to make your résumé more scannable:

1. Use plain, white résumé paper

2. Do not use any underlining or italicize any words

3. Do not use any graphics, tables, or charts

4. Use filled-in bullets or asterisks

5. Use Times New Roman, size 11 to 16 point

6. Do not use 10 point

ELECTRONIC

An electronic résumé is one that can be sent electronically. This means it can be sent in the body of an e-mail or through electronic résumé banks and job sites, such as **Monster.com**.

Résumés that are going to be sent this way can be created in different file formats. You might have heard the term ASCII, which stands for American Standard Code for Information Interchange. Experts recommend that electronic résumés use ASCII file formats, as they are universally recognized by the different computer systems. There are many different ASCII file formats, but the most common are plain text, rich text, and hypertext.

Plain text is the most popular format between computers. It is easy to identify by the .txt at the end of the file name. When you use this format, be aware that it looks plain. There cannot be any tabs or bullets. To compensate, you can use asterisks or another character to achieve a bulleted look.

Rich text format can be easily identified by the .rtf file extension at the end of the document name. This type of format allows more design options and is slowly becoming more popular for use between different computer systems. It works well for existing résumés that are in a Word document and that will be sent as an e-mail attachment. Be aware that there is a chance that some computers will not recognize this file format. Therefore, if you do not know about the computer that you are sending your résumé to, it is safer to send your résumés in a plain text format.

Hypertext can be identified by the file extension .htm or .html. As this is a Web page, the person reading your résumé needs to have a Web browser, like Internet Explorer, to view it.

Tips for writing this format include:

- Do not use special formatting or graphics

- Prepare in text-based format

- Include ten to twenty keywords from the job ad

ELECTRONIC — WITHIN THE BODY OF AN E-MAIL

Many times, employers and recruiters ask for your résumé to be cut and pasted into the body of an e-mail so they will not have the problems associated with attachments.

Follow these simple rules for a résumé that is going to be sent in the text of an e-mail message:

1. Do not use any tabs

2. Justify all the text to the left

3. Keep each line to 65 characters

4. Save your résumé in plain text format

WEB RÉSUMÉS

With the extensive technological advancement happening with Web site development, creating your own Web site has become easy. With this step comes the opportunity to develop a Web site résumé. This type of résumé is not right for everyone. However, if you are in a technological field where it would be advantageous to display your talents, or in an artistic field where it would help to show your creativity, it might be extremely appropriate to have. Anyone can have one, although it is not required, and it does show technological savvy and a willingness to stay up with current trends. Web résumés also offer the advantage of being available 24 hours a day for reviewing. If you do the Web site résumé properly, you provide an excellent interactive experience that will leave a recruiter feeling impressed and wanting more.

A Web résumé is visual and must engage the reader's attention immediately. The résumé must look professional and must provide the information that the reader is looking for. This type of résumé does not replace the paper version or, as it is also called, the presentation résumé; instead, it is used alongside the traditional version. All the same, writing points apply to a Web résumé.

- Put down an accomplishments or skills summary

- Incorporate all the keywords you can

- Make the information easily accessible to the reader

- Make the writing clear and concise

- Demonstrate your skills

There are three ways to create a Web résumé:

1. Do it yourself

2. Use an online résumé builder

3. Hire a professional

DO IT YOURSELF

If you already have software like FrontPage or Dreamweaver and the skills to use it, you already have what you need to build a Web site. If you do not have these skills or these programs, this is something you will need to consider getting. You will also need a place to put your résumé. Like anything that you need to post for someone to see, you need to have a location for your Web résumé.

Most Internet service providers (ISPs) offer a certain amount of space for you to post things to your Web site. Check with the ISP where you have an e-mail account to see how much space you are allowed.

If you already have a Web site, you can go ahead and create the new pages for your Web résumé.

USE AN ONLINE RÉSUMÉ-BUILDER

Technology, along with moving Web sites and résumés forward, has provided services to help you create a great résumé. There are several free online services — one example is Yahoo. Also, America Online offers this free service with a monthly subscription. There are budget sites that provide the same service for low costs of less than $40 per month. **CareerFolios. com** is one example where, for $39 per month, you can choose your design and colors, copy and paste your résumé information into online forms, and a Web résumé is automatically created for you using their templates.

HIRE A PROFESSIONAL

Not everyone has the time, talent, or the inclination to create their own Web résumé. For these people, hiring a professional may be the best option. There are several excellent professionals who design Web sites and Web résumés. Look for one who has a good reputation, references, and designs that you can see for yourself.

There are advantages and disadvantages to using a Web résumé. Let us look at both.

ADVANTAGES

Here are some of the advantages of a well-done Web site résumé:

- Provides a stronger impact than a traditional paper or text résumé

- Offers 24-hour availability

- Demonstrates visual proof of appreciation for technology

- Allows more information to be presented than a traditional résumé

- Can link to a portfolio, making your skills and abilities readily available

- May include video or audio material

- Allows you to present materials and links to important affiliations, awards given, and possible honors handed out

- Can be the size you need it to be instead of being restricted to one or two pages

- Can include actual references in audio format

- Allows you to apply your professional touch more clearly

DISADVANTAGES

For every advantage, there seems to be a disadvantage. Here are the problems to consider with Web site résumés:

- A Web résumé is a considerable investment

- It may not be something you can do yourself

- A considerable cost can be attached if you hire a professional

- There is a considerable learning curve involved if you are going to do it yourself

- If not done well, it will get you rejected based on the look of your site alone

- It will only reach recruiters who are willing to take this extra step

- If you use graphics or audio files that take time to load, recruiters may not wait for it to load

- Broken links and nonfunctioning audio files are common complaints of Web résumés

- Your Web site could go down at inconvenient times

- Much time is required to design and sort out what you want and need to put down

POINTS TO REMEMBER FOR YOUR WEB RÉSUMÉ

It does not matter whether you are doing your Web résumé on your own, online, or with the help of a professional; there are certain things that you do and do not want to do with this type of résumé.

Do

- Choose calm and quiet background colors. Preferably, use only one background color. You need to complement the colored hyperlinks and not have them blend away into nothing. Loud colors are not appropriate for that quiet, professional look.

- Use an easy-to-read, Web-friendly font. Good choices include Arial, Verdana, and the classic Times New Roman.

- Keep the formatting clean and simple. It is fine to use lines, tables, boxes, graphics, and even background colors and designs, in small doses. Like everything, you need to understand when enough is enough. If you overfill your Web résumé with these types of design features, you run the risk of turning away your reader. Keep it simple.

- Do not underline. Hyperlinks are underlined, so do not underline your text.

- Check that your e-mail address is active. If you are using a "mailto" link, check that it is working. You want this link to automatically open the person's e-mail program to allow them to write you a message.

- Use an easy-to-use navigation system. Popular systems include a menu on the left-hand side of the page or a menu bar across the top where there are links that will direct the reader to the different sections of your résumé. These sections can include Work Experience, Education, and Awards.

- Along with the navigation issue, make sure all links in the text are clearly visible. A recruiter will not hunt for the links to move where they need to go. It helps to make the links a different color once clicked. Help the reader see where they have been.

- If you are doing one long Web page résumé instead of several linked pages, make sure you give the reader a way back up to the top of the page. This is usually in the form of a "back to the top" link after every section.

Do Not

Just as there are things to make sure you do, there are specific things you should not do with a Web résumé:

- Do not overdo the amount of hyperlinks, particularly when these links take the reader off your Web site.

- Do not put in large graphics that take a long time to load.

- Do not overuse italics or bold lettering. This use of all capital letters is considered "shouting" and should be avoided at all times.

- Do not use material, text, or graphics that you do not have permission to use. Copyright laws apply to your Web site résumé and your Web site.

- Do not fill the screen with continuous text. As with your paper résumé, you should make good use of white space on your Web résumé. This makes the résumé easier to read.

- Do not send out cover letters or paper résumés that show the link for your Web résumé until it is up and ready for viewing.

THE RIGHT IMAGE

A professional image is important, and with a Web résumé you have an excellent opportunity to project the right image. The Internet is an overwhelming blend of colors and images. Do not make your résumé blend into the mess. Just because there are many colors, graphics, cartoons, backgrounds, add-ons, and special effects that you could use, this does not mean that you should.

Professional image means:

- Use color sparingly. It is fine on headings and for a spot of color. Overdoing it will give your résumé an amateurish look.

- Keep the visuals simple. If you are putting in graphics, keep the background clean, simple, and not textured. If you are using colored text, consider a white background. Keep the creativity in check, unless you are in a creative industry.

- One of the biggest deterrents to a professional look is the additions of your local weather, daily horoscopes, or sales ads. A Web résumé is to show your skills and experience and to provide access to supporting information. It is not the place to show family photos.

- Business graphics can be a good addition, if they are pertinent to your industry. Do not use animation or large files.

- Make sure all text is edited, proofread, and says exactly what needs to be said and not one word more. There is nothing professional about sloppy grammar and spelling mistakes on your Web résumé.

Remember to balance text versus white space, graphics versus color, and especially, appearance with professionalism.

YOU HAVE YOUR WEB RÉSUMÉ — NOW WHAT?

If you choose to create a Web résumé, when you send out a cover letter or paper résumé inviting a recruiter to view your Web résumé, you need to present it as an opportunity to learn more rather than a duplicate of material already presented. This is an opportunity for a recruiter or hiring manager to learn more. Do not just add your URL (Web site address) at the top with all your contact information, like your name and phone number; put it in the text along with a statement to intrigue the reader.

Consider putting in a statement like this:

- Clips from a recent sales managers' presentation can be viewed at my Web résumé, **www.yourWeb site.com.**

- To view my recent awards from the Emily Carr Institute of Art, visit my Web site at **www.yourWeb site.com.**

Besides pointedly directing a potential employer to your Web site, you need to consider registering your Web site with a search engine. Some of these registration services are free, like Google, but many are fee-based. Consider placing your URL as part of your signature on all outgoing e-mails and paper materials, like business cards, letterhead, and business envelopes.

VIDEO RÉSUMÉ

The jury is out as to whether video résumés are "in" or "out" for today's job seeker. From the increasing number of them posted on places like **YouTube.com**, they appear to be in.

Your résumé is a marketing tool; it is selling you and your skills. Some people are never "on," while many others are never "off." We all know people like that. They are the life of the party. They are the ones that have an answer for everything. But they are not necessarily the ones who should be doing video résumés.

You do not have to be a comedian or a showman to create and execute a professional video résumé. On the contrary, confidence in yourself and your abilities is all that is required.

However, just because you can does not mean you should.

Let us take a closer look at video résumés.

ADVANTAGES

- Short video résumés, between one and three minutes, are an excellent marketing tool to go with your traditional résumé — if they are well done. However, if you are planning to read off your résumé or do clown tricks while pointing out your skills, do not bother — unless, of course, you are applying for a position working as a clown.

- These types of videos are more common in professions where appearance and physical skills are qualifications. These types of occupations include singing, dancing, and acting.

- When they first emerged, video résumés were a fad that seemed to die quickly, partly because no one really knew what to do with this new media. It was not recognized for the potentially valuable marketing tool it is. Like most technology, this has finally found acceptance with some and is making a strong comeback.

Some information technology professionals are using this media to showcase their graphic design, animation, and programming skills. When combined with a serious effort at addressing the common myths about "geeks," this media can pack a powerful punch. The outdated myths are, of course, that these people lack communication skills, social skills, and are prone to interpersonal relationship problems. With a video résumé, these talented professionals have a chance to show personality and professional communication ability and blow the myths away.

If you are not able or willing to take the time to learn how to create a video yourself, there are many companies that specialize in creating Web résumés. They can help you create a résumé reflective of your profession and the occupation you are interested in. This service can be expensive and can cost several hundred dollars or more, depending on the extras you require.

Some components of a video résumé that need to be decided on are music, logos, special effects, and a Web space to host your video résumé.

There is also help available from several video résumé wizards you can use that allow you to follow the process with simple step-by-step instructions, often for less than $20.

DISADVANTAGES

As with every media and résumé format, there are specific disadvantages to each. Here are some of the problems with video résumés:

- The hiring manager or recruiter has to have the time or the willingness to watch the video

- The company might not have the technology to watch the video, a slow Internet connection, or browsers that are not compatible

- The lack of proven guidelines in the industry to know what belongs on a video résumé

- The potential to overdo a video résumé makes this a difficult media to control

VIDEO RÉSUMÉ TECHNIQUES

To present a professional video résumé, learning a couple of these techniques will help.

- Use a short, concise introduction. Introduce yourself and what you are doing.

- Include a short closing that provides your contact information.

- If distributing the video, get copies made professionally. Label each copy with a clean, business-like label. Include your contact information and a written résumé.

- Use résumé videos for contacting employers who are not in the same town. This type of résumé is not intended to replace a face-to-face interview. Being called in for an interview is the goal of any résumé, including a video résumé.

- Speak at a normal speed and enunciate your words clearly.

- Do not read from a script; if you need cue cards, have them where you can see them off camera. Do not hold papers in your hands.

- Practice. When people are put in front of a camera, many mannerisms are highlighted that would not be normally seen. Flipping your hair, rubbing your nose, and making odd quirks with your mouth are common. Practice helps to minimize these obvious nervous characteristics.

- Be critical. Watch your first attempt at making a professional video résumé and do a critique. Should you animate your face a little more or a little less? Do you need to stop waving your hands? Are you wearing appropriate clothing?

- Show the video to your friends and listen to their constructive comments. In the end, it has to represent you.

Some professionals are using the opportunity of creating a video résumé to answer potential interview questions. There is plenty of research available on potential interview questions. Practice your answers, then practice them in front of the video camera.

Because today's graduates have casual technological skills, software that is increasingly easier to use, and the availability to post videos and access millions of potential employers on places like YouTube, the practice of using video résumés is likely to explode.

RECRUITMENT VIDEOS

With the popular movement of video résumés on the Internet, it is no surprise that recruitment videos, although not new, are also becoming popular. This is a great way to get an inside look at the way a company works, the general ages of the staff, and the dress code. This obviously is only a glimpse and does not replace a proper interview. It is also important to realize that these videos are only going to show you the good things and not the bad things about the company. The videos have a marketing sales overview to them, as they are trying to sell the company. The rules are simple; if the video intrigues you, do your research before you go send your application in for consideration. It is safer to do your work first than try to correct the mistake after you have been hired.

CASE STUDY: JANICE WORTHINGTON

Janice Worthington, Certified Professional Résumé Writer and Job Search Coach, is founder and president of Worthington Career Services, one of the most prominent career coaching and résumé preparation firms in the U.S. For over 35 years, Janice has helped thousands of people in every aspect of the job-hunting industry. In 1999, she was honored as a Top 10 Industry Leader by The Professional Association of Résumé Writers and Career Coaches.

She started as an executive recruiter and found it difficult to watch wonderfully qualified clients do poorly on interviewing and testing. So in 1987, she left the company to become a candidate advocate, coaching others to develop skill perception and the qualifications to go up against recruiters and HR personnel. She wanted to be able to help everyone, so her family business now works for the needs of every industry.

She describes the changes in the industry. "We used to teach people that a career was much like a train you got on and stayed on. Then it became more like a bus, with one or two transfers, and then it became like a car, with you becoming the driver. Finally, it is like an ATV, and you can get off the road and take it where you want to."

Her philosophy is that the résumé is just one piece of the hiring process, and all of it is dependent on the job market, which is dependent on the economy. Résumés became tools, and then interviews. Since the millennium, because of the industry, the hiring process has changed. Employers are not willing to see as many people. They also want more information up front. So now, her company produces three- or four-page résumés. Today, everyone needs a résumé; twenty years ago, the basic clerical staff did not need a résumé.

CASE STUDY: JANICE WORTHINGTON

Several things are influencing the hiring methodology today; we have four decades of workers in the workforce today, the largest talent pool and the largest selection of talent. Many seniors are not retiring, or are coming back.

Her philosophy is that your résumé should answer these questions:

1. Who are you?

2. What do you want?

3. What have you got?

4. Where do you work?

5. What do they do

6. What do you do?

7. Are you any good?

8. Prove it.

Janice offers the following advice to today's job hunters:

1. You are not less of an applicant if you are unemployed. You have not been devalued because you have been downsized.

2. You are not alone. Go to your flock and you will feel better.

3. Get momentum going and do not stop. Do not let a day go by without doing a job search activity.

4. She has never found anyone who could not get a job if they were prepared to do what was required.

5. Control the degree of discouragement; keep positive.

She believes that you, as a job hunter, have far more control than you think. You have far more to offer than you believe. Most of all, believe in yourself.

*Janice can be reached at Worthington Career Services **www.worthingtoncareers. com** and **www.worthingtonresumes.com**, 6636 Belleshire Street, Columbus, Ohio 43229, 614-890-1645, (877) 9-Resume (877-973-7863) or by e-mail at Janice@ WorthingtonResumes.com.*

CHAPTER 5:

THE PARTS AND PIECES

The sum of a résumé is only as good as the individual parts. Each area deserves your full attention, and each area should be focused on the job you are applying for and your stated objective.

This chapter includes an overview of each of the main parts of a résumé, followed by a discussion of each section and the details of what needs to be covered and why.

These discussions cover:

- Name and Contact Information

- Career Goal or Objective

- Career Summary/Professional Summary

- Employment History

- Education History

- Professional Associations

- Personal Information

- References

- Less Common Sections

NAME AND CONTACT INFORMATION

At the top of the page, you need to have your full name as it appears on your academic records or any other documentation that the recruiters and managers may want to see. You do not want there to be any confusion as to who owns the documents. If you go by a middle name or a nickname, you can put the shortened name in brackets where it belongs, such as Stephen Percival (Percy) Howard or Kathryn (Cat) Anne Brewster.

Include your full address and phone number. If you are teaching or working, you can put down the school and business contact information on your résumé. Make sure being contacted about another job while working at your current job is something you want to have happen. It may be months before you are contacted, so make sure the information you put down is valid. You want it to be easy for a prospective employer to contact you.

Put down your main e-mail address where you can be contacted. Do not list two or three e-mails. Only list the one you will be checking on a regular basis. Make sure the e-mail address is a professional-sounding one. Just because we can have cute or unique e-mail addresses does not mean they are the best idea for a résumé. Your e-mail **puuurfectlysweet@hotmail.com** belongs between you and your friends.

Do not put down a URL or Web address for a personal Web site unless it is a business/professional Web site. Students will often put down personal sites that contain inappropriate material. Recruiters are looking for ways to discard résumés — and this is a great way for them to decide you are not mature enough to be hired.

Include your Web address if this is where you keep:

- An online résumé (up-to-date version)

- Copies of reference letters, certifications, or other documents that are relevant to your job search

- Professional or academic papers, abstracts, list of professional papers, or presentations

- Portfolio containing photos you have taken, artwork, or other creative material relevant for the job you are applying for. These items can take a long time to load and may result in the viewer clicking away from your site.

- Writing samples, if pertinent to the position to which you are applying

- Samples of Web development work, if this is appropriate for the job

HEADER WORKSHEET

Header

Name (as you want it to be on your résumé)

Address

City   **State**   **ZIP**

Phone Number (number where an employer could call and leave a message)

E-mail Address

Web Site (Only if appropriate)

When it is done, it will look something like this:

John Doe
241 Sahomish Dr.
Seattle, WA 98188
Phone: 206-555-3333
jdoe@hotmail.com

If you need to have two addresses, one way to do this is shown below:

John Doe
241 Sahomish Dr.
Seattle, WA 98188
Phone: 206-555-3333

John Doe
422 Oregon Way
Amarillo, TX 79101
Phone: 806-555-3333

Alternatively, you can put your address(es) at the bottom of the page in the footer, like this:

John Doe, 241 Sahomish Dr., Seattle, WA 98188, Phone: 206-555-3333

Note: This is the first impression a prospective employer will have of you. Be true to your profession here. Creativity is allowed if creativity is a qualification. Otherwise, stay conservative and professional.

CAREER GOAL OR OBJECTIVE

There is much controversy over including a career objective on your résumé today. It is considered old-fashioned by some and standard by others. If you choose to include this type of statement, it is important to understand what purpose it plays in your résumé.

It is intended to tell the prospective employer the type of work you are looking for. This sets the tone for the rest of the information that follows, which should support the listed objective. Make it clear and simple. Do not go overboard and try to tell a story. If you are sending a résumé to support an application for scholarship or graduate school, state that here.

When writing a career goal or objective, follow these simple rules:

- Make sure to put down the industry you want to work in or the type of work you want to do. Also, depending on the job, you could put down the type of specialized skill you want to apply. Example: Media liaison position, interested in using public speaking skills.

- Avoid generalities, like "a position where I can use my skills and abilities." This means nothing if you do not specify your skills and abilities. Do not say that you are interested in a job related to an industry or specialty, like business or science. That is too broad. Make it more specific.

- If you have several different objectives, create different résumés showing each variation. Twist the rest of the résumé to support the variation.

If you are wondering what to use instead of a career goal or objective, some specialists in the field are suggesting you include a "positioning statement."

POSITIONING STATEMENT

Louise Fletcher is an industry specialist with over 15 years of experience and the cofounder and president of **BlueskyResumes.com**. In her article, "How to Write a Résumé That Gets Results," she writes that recruiters and hiring managers do not like résumé goals and objectives because they focus on the needs of the job seeker instead of the needs of the employer. She uses this example: "Seeking a software engineer position with a progressive employer where I can contribute to the development of new technologies and work with bright, committed people."

She says this may be honest, but only addresses what you want and what you have to offer. Her suggestion is something like this: "Software engineer with seven years experience developing leading-edge technologies."

Now the reader can see what you have to offer. Fletcher also suggests that you tailor this statement for each position to highlight the connection between what the company needs and what you have to offer.

PROFILE, PROFESSIONAL SUMMARY

To focus your résumé on your skills and accomplishments, consider adding a section called a Summary or Profile. This powerful opening draws a reader in, displays your best selling point, and demonstrates your value as a candidate.

There are many different names for this type of section. For example:

- Profile

- Professional Profile

- Professional Summary

- Summary of Qualifications

- Summary

- Expertise

Choose the one that suits your skills and professional accomplishments. Include in this section at least some of the following:

- Who you are

- Title/level of current position

- Number of years of experience (if longer than 15 years, put 15+)

- Areas of expertise/strengths/specialization

- Accomplishment highlights

- Skills/experience that add to your value, especially when they are unexpected

- Any advanced degrees, certifications, or licenses

- Languages, if relevant

- Technical/computer skills (only if not in IT)

- Facts and figures whenever possible (budget managed/revenue generated/client accounts/money saved)

- Top business skills

- Awards earned, if relevant, will receive more attention if listed here

- Keywords and industry buzzwords

- List any affiliations, but only if they are pertinent to the job

- List major projects you have been involved in

- Special awards pertinent to the job

- Be specific

Do Not:

- Be vague

- Talk about career aspirations

- List desired salary and perks

Here is an example of one point that could be put in this section and a rewrite with more detail to show you the difference.

This is a common statement type seen by many hiring managers:

> *Increased sales by 15% through new advertising campaign.*

This statement is a classic "so what?" Without more information, you have no way to measure this 15 percent increase. Perhaps in the previous two years, the company has had 35 percent increases.

Now look at this version:

> *Created new marketing directive, changed service providers, and drove sales forward 15% after two years of sales decline.*

If you have more information that strengthens your position, put it down:

> *Created new marketing directive, changed service providers, and drove sales forward 15% after two years of sales decline. Increase was achieved in spite of market downfall.*

This section is your 15- to 30-second shot at fame; get it right and you will have a good chance of winning a job interview.

When you are trying to define your accomplishments, ask yourself these questions:

1. What sets you apart from the competition?

2. How did you do a better job than a competitor did?

3. What were the challenges you faced?

4. What did you do to overcome them?

5. What were the results?

Also, consider what you did for the company to:

- Make or save money

- Save time

- Solve a problem

- Increase sales

These types of answers will grab the reader's attention and win you the job interview.

EMPLOYMENT HISTORY

This is another important part of your résumé. This is where a recruiter automatically looks to see the kind of work you have done, for whom, and when.

You need to make your work experience support your goal or positioning statement. This work experience does not have to be paid experience. It can include an internship, volunteer work, or club association work.

If you do not have related experience, it is important to list your employment history. It does show basic skills and work ethics, including skills that we rarely think about, like getting along with coworkers, time management, and meeting deadlines.

For each entry, list the job title, name and location of the organization, the dates that you worked for the company, and a description of your accomplishments during your time with that company. In this section, it is common to use phrases instead of writing out full sentences. They should be short and concise so you are presenting the important information and not wasting anyone's time.

Go as far back as is relevant to the job to which you are applying. Normally, your work history should go back ten to fifteen years.

Traditionally, this section is written using reverse chronological order. Begin with your last position and move on to the one before that, even if it was with the same company. For each position list:

- **Header:** Job title, company name, city, state, and the dates that you were in that position.

- **Description:** Include accomplishments achieved, contributions made, software and equipment used, and special projects you were involved with. Try to start with an action verb.

- **Training:** List any related training, including licensure and company seminars.

- **Recognition:** List any awards or special recognition received while in this position. You can include committees and company events, if pertinent to the job.

Note: List all jobs, even part-time jobs. Keep the language tight and use action-oriented wording.

Do not try to make complete, coherent sentences at this point. This part of the worksheet is for getting the ideas down.

EMPLOYMENT HISTORY WORKSHEET PART 1

Header: _____   _____

           Job Title   Company Name

_____   _____   _____

           City   State   Dates

Description:

_____

_____

Training:

_____

_____

Recognition:

_____

_____

At this stage, look at what you have written above and try to refine it to say exactly what needs to be said, with the least amount of words possible. Verify that you have used action-oriented wording. Refer to Chapter 7.

EMPLOYMENT HISTORY WORKSHEET PART 2

Description:

_____

_____

Training:

_____

_____

Recognition:

_____

_____

Now, leave this section and come back to it later. When you read it again, you will be able to get a better impression of how you did. Taking a break will also help your creativity kick in and give you more ideas of how to present yourself.

DATES

Dates are a simple part of a résumé, but for some people, they create havoc. Not everyone's work history has a nice, consistent, chronological explanation.

The solution is to give the same emphasis to the dates as you do all the rest of the information on your résumé. If your dates are clear and consistent and are something you want to bring to the manager's attention, put down full dates. If you have gaps in your employment history and do not want to bring attention to them, make the dates less obvious.

If you choose, you can put down just the number of years you worked at a place instead of listing the dates themselves. It may, however, give the impression you are hiding something.

Your age may be another reason for not wanting to put down dates. Education dates from 40 years ago make the math easy to work out. When listing your education, you can choose not to put down dates. If your work experience list has all the dates, your education dates do not matter as much, and you can leave them off without raising eyebrows.

Be honest and accurate when listing your dates. Recruiters check dates with your references and previous employers. You do not want to lose a job because of sloppiness or misleading dates.

There is no preferred method for the way you write the dates; just be consistent in your usage.

Putting dates on the left gives them a higher level of importance, as people read from left to right. You can also create a column to the far right of your résumé and list all dates there. This makes the dates easy to find. Do not use this method if you are creating a scannable résumé.

When listing dates, you may use months and years, or years only. This will depend partly on the space you have available and how comfortable you are with the dates you have to list. Space is short, so writing out the months will take up valuable space. For that reason, consider using an abbreviation, like Feb. 2007, or the numerical value of 2/07. List both sides of a term the same, such as:

February 2001 to March 2004

Feb. 2001 – Mar. 2004

Feb 2001 – Mar 2004

2/01 – 3/04

You can use a dotted line to draw the eye across the page to the dates on a standard résumé. Do not use this format on a scannable résumé.

EDUCATIONAL HISTORY

The résumé format dictates whether education or experience comes first. It does not matter which you choose. What is important is what you include in this section. Below is a list of items to include:

- List degree(s) in the order of most recent. This includes degrees you have earned and those you are in the process of earning.

    a) Also, with each degree, list the level and major (second major, minor, or even concentration). Try to keep the material contained on one line, if possible.

    b) On the second line, include the institution and city/state. Put down the university's full name, and if the institute has a common short name, put that name in brackets after the official name. An example is Simon Fraser University (SFU). This will depend on the type of employer and whether you think they would be familiar with the university name.

- List additional degrees and education levels in reverse chronological order — meaning most recent degree first.

- You can list the degree in bold lettering to highlight your educational accomplishment.

- If you studied abroad, make sure you include that here as well.

- Include career advancement course work.

- Add in any pertinent independent studies.

Do not include your high school education if you are a working adult. If you have a degree, a high school diploma was required to get there. By the time you get to graduate school, you should only list college and graduate level work. The exception would be if you have a diploma in a subject that directly relates to the job and is different from the college stream.

EDUCATION WORKSHEET
List degrees and certifications that you have and any pertinent course work that you did. List by most recent; include the program, school, city, and dates attended.

1._____
Degree or Certificate

_____
Majors/Minors or Course Highlights

_____
School Name, City/State   Year graduated or years enrolled

_____
Courses relevant to goal

2._____
Degree or Certificate

_____
Majors/Minors or Course Highlights

_____
School Name, City/State   Year graduated or years enrolled

_____
Courses relevant to job goal

EDUCATION WORKSHEET
3._____ Degree or Certificate
_____ Majors/Minors or Course Highlights
_____ School Name, City/State   Year graduated or years enrolled
_____ Courses relevant to job goal

PROFESSIONAL ASSOCIATIONS

When listing the organizations that you belong to, use the complete name, not just the abbreviation or acronym. Again, you are trying to make your résumé simple and easy to read.

- Include a simple explanation of the nature of the organization if it is not obvious from the name.

- Do not include that you are a "member of" the organization. If you are listing it, you are a member. Therefore, do not list the organization unless you are a member.

- If you held an office in an organization, include the position information. Briefly list your accomplishments as you did earlier in your résumé under work experience. Take this opportunity to list activities and skills that support your application.

- Do not list activities unless they apply to the position. You can expand on this information during a job interview.

- Leave off political or religious associations. You may be proud of your contributions, but you do not want to run the risk of alienating someone before you even have a chance to talk to them.

- If you belong to many associations, list only the most important.

MEMBERSHIPS

List professional groups/organizations that you belong to, including dates and positions you have held.

_____

_____

_____

SKILLS

Almost every traditional résumé has a skill section of some kind. This could be a general heading, called "Skills," or it could be a heading directed to a specific group of skills, such as "Computer Skills" or "Foreign Language Skills." How you title this section will depend on the skills you have to offer and the skills the prospective employer is requesting.

If you have several different skills, use the general heading of "Skills," but feel free to add in subheadings for clarity.

You need to have an idea of your strengths and abilities, and the material from Chapter 2 can help. Look at the worksheets you completed. Look at the job description, then look at your list of work experiences.

- What stands out?

- What is the most important thing the prospective employer will need to know about you?

- What traits will give you an edge over the competition?

- What skills can you take from another job to this one?

NOW, PUT IT ALL TOGETHER

Write down the top reasons why you should get the job. Try to list five. Again, do not worry about full sentences. Focus on getting down the ideas. Think in terms of the job ad; what is on their shopping list for the new employee to have? Now, try to create a list of your own that matches the ad from your own experience. Think about the years of experience you have to offer, special licenses or training, achievements, recognition, and transferable skills.

_____

_____

_____

_____

_____

Now, organize your skills and accomplishments into groups that a recruiter can easily identify. This includes clerical, managerial, supervisory, and personnel. Then, take each one and add the details. For example:

Supervisory — Ten years, supervised 30 technicians, handled budget and training

Skill Category	Details
_____	_____
_____	_____
_____	_____
_____	_____

Now, refine your statements to create more impact and to decrease unnecessary wording.

_____

_____

_____

Now, list any organizations you spent time volunteering with. Include what you did, the organization's name, location, and the time you spent with the organization. It might be necessary to write a short description to have the reader understand your role, especially if special training was required.

_____

_____

_____

CHAPTER 6:

BRANDING

This term is more normally applied to large corporations and name-brand products. It is the way that a company or a product is presented to the world in order to have it quickly recognized. When a person is asked to think of a name of an automobile, they might be quick to answer "Ford." There are many other equally good automobile companies, but few that have managed to have their name so prominent in the minds of the public. That is branding on a corporate level.

In the job-hunting industry, this term is used on a more personal and individual level. Its use is quickly becoming commonplace, and it is important to understand what it is and how it can help you. It is not mandatory to use branding to get a wonderful job, but it would not hurt. If, after reading this and doing more research on your own, you decide this is not for you, then let it go. If, however, the concept is intriguing, then look into it a bit more and consider how personal branding can help you.

Examples of people with good personal branding are Oprah Winfrey and Tiger Woods. You do not need to be a celebrity to do the same. Consider that a personal brand helps you to stand out from the crowd, especially if you are looking for a job out of a large pool of possible candidates.

If you are considering this type of marketing, here a few reasons to look at creating and implementing personal branding strategies:

- It can help to set you apart, as this is still a relatively new idea

- It allows you to show your skills and personality in a unique way

- It helps to establish and increase your reputation and integrity

- It helps you to establish a presence and a ladder of success

Thomas Murrell, in his article, "The Power of Personal Branding Strategies," talks about personal branding operating on several different levels, with the first level being your inner core personal brand that is shaped by your beginnings. The second level is your created personal brand. This level is the process of self development that has built your skills and knowledge to create the person you are. The third level is the outer level, or as he calls it, the perceived personal brand. He talks about how you can shape other people's perceptions by managing the way other people see you.

To do this effectively, it helps to have a role where you are speaking, writing, or communicating in some way that gets you noticed. The brand you establish has to be repeated constantly. It needs to be reinforced with the clothes you wear, the places you go, the words you speak, and especially by your actions.

This is much easier to do in a visible role. If you are talked about, read about, seen about, or heard about, then people believe that you must know your stuff and that you are better than those others that they do not hear about.

That is why your actions are so important. It can take years to build up personal brands, but poor actions on your part can destroy your brand or your name in seconds.

Paul Copcutt of Square Peg Solutions says, "For many years now, the vast majority of positions are being filled through referrals and networking, and certainly in the current world of talent shortage, employee referral is a rapidly growing source of new hires for many companies — as high as 50 percent in some cases."

That is where the use of personal branding can come in. It can be used to create different career marketing documents as a door opens, giving the job seeker time, and hopefully greater knowledge, to follow up with a targeted résumé once specifics of a position or openings are known.

BRANDED BIO

For the job hunter of today, Paul Copcutt suggests avoiding the cookie-cutter résumé and putting in as much of your specific skills and experience that are relevant to the position as possible. This can only come from having a clear understanding of the role in question.

Gather as much information as possible, starting with the job ad; but with as much as 50 percent of the job market coming through networking and referrals, sometimes a company has not even gotten around to posting the position anywhere. If there is no job description, try to get a conversation with either the HR manager or, ideally, the hiring manager. If you can talk to an incumbent, that would be ideal. Once you have as much information as you can get, you need to put together a résumé.

Using feedback about differentiating attributes and strengths and merging that with a high-level view of your work experience, you can craft a one-page branded biography. That gives the reader a good sense of who you are, where you have been, and what you have done without the preconceptions of how long you were at company XYZ or why you took a drop in job title after leaving.

This should be a one- to two-page document that gives a clear but general overview of your experience and background. Typically, these documents are written in the third person.

The bio can replace the need to post a résumé on job boards, retaining your control over who gets to see your résumé, when, and more importantly, what it contains.

SAMPLE OF BRANDED BIO

Paul Copcutt
1063 King Street West, Ste 412
Hamilton, ON L8S 4S3
Tel: 905-628-1100
E-mail: paul@squarepegsolution.com

CAREER PROFILE

Paul Copcutt is an experienced and credible senior business development and marketing executive with more than 15 years at one of Canada's most respected medical industry companies, Evolution Healthcare. His work assignments have included roles in Toronto, nationally across Canada, as well as connections internationally in the USA and beyond.

Paul has developed exceptionally strong strategic relationship-building skills that have generated impressive sales accomplishments across a number of sectors, diverse customer profiles, and business environments. He is comfortable working at any organizational level, but has spent the last six years leading teams that are working with senior healthcare leaders in major hospitals. He has spearheaded the sales and marketing efforts for Evolution that have generated significant exposure and required a creative approach with strong leadership and team collaboration skills.

Paul excels at opportunities where he can position the benefits of working with a company by building credibility and value in their offering and leveraging resources to increase perceived customer value, thereby creating a competitive advantage. He enjoys taking charge of an opportunity and leading a multifunctional team to a successful outcome. However, his experience also has involved full P&L focus, requiring him to be both a strategic thinker and someone who can assess a situation, identify key issues and priorities, and develop methods and processes to critically analyze information, prepare and present succinct reports, and lead action.

In addition to his business accomplishments, Paul is a graduate from the University of London and has been identified to attend key global management and leadership programs, both internally and externally. He is a highly energetic and driven business professional who quickly adapts to meet new business challenges. He is extremely customer focused, an effective and engaging communicator, and an individual capable of making significant and continuing business contributions.

Paul expects to continue to focus his career in the health sector, where he has achieved a great deal and is viewed by many as a key leader and partner. He is also very comfortable working with all types of healthcare providers (public or private) and clinicians and has led government relations both nationally and provincially for the last two years.

SAMPLE OF BRANDED BIO

His skills and experience, however, are certainly transferable to a number of other industries where change is occurring and there is a need to view the sales and marketing process and customer relationship strategically and support actionable processes and plans.

A successful and ambitious individual, he is seeking a senior VP or C-level role with a company that is regarded as a leader in the field, medium to large in size, highly customer focused, a work culture committed to continuous improvement, and a company that offers future career possibilities. The role will require a high degree of relationship building, positioning high-value solutions, will provide opportunities to lead initiatives, and most likely involve a North American focus.

(This branded bio was supplied by Paul Copcutt of Square Peg Solution.)

BRAND SKILLS SHEET

After a branded bio, consider adding a brand skills sheet to add extra information and examples of your abilities and skills.

You can do analysis and, through the use of specific assessments and feedback groups, you can identify what your peers and colleagues, managers, and even friends and clients perceive as your key brand skills.

Then you can take these top skills and develop your brand stories around how you have used those brand skills in specific job situations with measurable results.

This "brag" sheet gives the reader a real flavor for who you are, what you might bring to their company, and how you have been successful in the past. Many hiring managers believe that the best predictor of future success is past accomplishments, and you are giving them examples of these achievements.

Your accomplishments should use as much relevant information as possible, without compromising confidentiality, while trying to make it as measurable as possible.

SAMPLE OF KEY STRENGTH SUMMARY (BRANDED SKILLS SHEET)

Paul Copcutt
1063 King Street West, Ste. 412
Hamilton, ON L8S 4S3
Tel: 905-628-1100
E-mail: paul@squarepegsolution.com

KEY STRENGTHS SUMMARY

Maximizer — Focus on strengths as a way to stimulate personal and group excellence. Seek to transform something strong into something superb.

As a sales manager with Boots Industries, I was responsible for a national team of nine who achieved overall country performance at 25% over budget two years running. We were able to meet the challenge of incorporating capital equipment sales into a business where disposable sales were the focus, increasing revenues in both areas.

A practical example: Chose the top performers in each area of sales (disposable and capital equipment) and had each of them present their sales methods to the group during a national sales meeting. Also established a system of biweekly telephone meetings where each sales representative could share successes, ask for input on how to overcome challenges within their territories, and encourage each other to succeed.

Strategic — Create alternative ways to proceed. Given any scenario can quickly spot the relevant patterns and issues.

At ABC Consulting as Senior Client Services Director, I was responsible for a budget in excess of $6 million providing pharmaceutical marketing expertise to global and U.S. brand teams on such products as Xyzerpa, Nomikal, and Verdunne. The role required building consensus between brand teams and individuals in global head offices and country branches and creating benchmarks for and delivering ROI for programs that impacted the bottom line of both areas. This was a new service we were delivering, and as the relationship progressed, we worked with the customer to create ROI that allowed them to continue to justify allocating budget to funding the programs. Funding was shared between global teams and country brand teams, so we had to provide the ROI to the global team so that they could sell it to country brand teams; i.e., medical education Web casts featuring key opinion leaders were developed and disseminated to physician audiences within each country. One of the ROIs we were able to establish, ensuring that over 50 percent of physician audience watched at least the first 30 seconds of the presentation. The program was built to ensure that the main message was included in those first 30 seconds and the method of delivery — Web cast, e-mail newsletters, mailings, conference presentations— maximized exposure to the appropriate audience. We also worked on getting a physician database that was stellar, pertinent, and of high value to the client.

SAMPLE OF KEY STRENGTH SUMMARY (BRANDED SKILLS SHEET)

Input — A craving to know more. Often like to collect and archive all kinds of information.

Generally, I have a strong belief in continuous development and improvement, which I have followed throughout my career. I believe that this desire for more information makes me a highly efficient, results-driven, and challenge-driven professional with an exemplary background in developing and implementing new methods of marketing to healthcare professionals, and helps me to be an empathetic coach who works with people in an ongoing partnership designed to help produce win-win results.

I am regularly contacted by my network to provide input and reference to various resources as they consistently see me as a provider of value-added material and information and have come to rely on me for the knowledge.

Ideation — Fascinated by ideas. Able to find connections between seemingly disparate phenomena.

I am a conceptual and creative worker who is able to develop methods and processes to critically analyze information and prepare and present succinct reports, such as when I was asked to prepare reports for each of the countries (USA, Italy, France, Germany, UK, Spain, Puerto Rico, Switzerland, and Canada) who were involved with a multilanguage program involving five key opinion leaders presenting clinical findings on the use of Verdunne. This was the first time a program of this magnitude was undertaken, requiring the translation of all materials, Web casts, slide presentations, and marketing material disseminated on the Internet and by mail (print and CD-ROMs). The program required weekly tracking of all components as they were being developed and reports on these developments were to be sent to Pikco, Inc. brand marketing teams. Ongoing programs were also developed to track results on readership at launch, and weekly after this to three months post-launch.

Connectedness — Faith is the link between all things. There are few coincidences and almost every event has a reason.

When Polsocorp sold the Dentum division to Boots Industries and I went with the division to Boots to head up that division and create a smooth transition for the team at Boots (disposable to capital equipment sales), I realized that it was vital to keep connected and maintain relationships with customers who had been purchasing Dentum infusion pumps. One of our biggest customers was Carefull (a company providing home-infusion services and pharmacy services). There was no relationship between Boots Industries and Carefull and there was a sense of wariness on both sides. Within the first three months of the purchase of Dentum by Boots I organized a national sales meeting, bringing in all the Boots representatives from across Canada to Toronto.

SAMPLE OF KEY STRENGTH SUMMARY (BRANDED SKILLS SHEET)

I delivered training on the use and sales methods for the infusion pumps, highlighting the difference between disposable sales and capital equipment sales.

I presented research data that I had compiled by a third-party marketing firm showing current market analysis of infusion pump penetration in Canada and potential for sales over the next five years. I also invited the vice president and the director of pharmacy services from Carefull to present to the group, highlighting their services, their relationship with Polsocorp Dentum, and how they perceived our working relationship ongoing.

This sample was provided by Paul Copcutt of Square Peg Solution.

CASE STUDY FOR PAUL COPCUTT

Paul Copcutt is Canada's leading personal brand consultant, combining a passion for people with a realization that strengths and specialization are the keys to success; he guides his clients to that outcome.

As an experienced senior business development and marketing executive, he served for more than 15 years in the medical industry, at which time he decided to put into action a business plan he had written about starting a full-service talent services firm with recruitment, career-coaching incorporating personal branding and outsourced HR services.

He launched Square Peg Solution shortly after and quickly positioned his company as the world's first personal brand agency, working with women entrepreneurs and executives and the corporations who sell to them. They are deemed winners through the power of their networks, the quality of work they do, and their leadership acumen. He steps in when these women are ready to move up to the next level and crystallize their brands.

Over the years, Paul has seen a number of changes in the job industry. Companies are suffering from a talent shortage; as a result, they are more discerning as to who may join their teams. People must present themselves as unique or value-added to those potential employers in order to capitalize on such opportunities. In addition, companies are more judicious as to whom they give business; that is why business owners need to present a more credible and visible brand.

CASE STUDY FOR PAUL COPCUTT

As more people who were born into technology hit the job market, the need to manage and develop your online identity will become more prominent because companies and recruiters rely more heavily on the Internet to attract suitable candidates or hire prospective suppliers.

In order to maximize your résumé, he suggests making it differentiated and innovated. Include key contact details, make it easy to read and navigate, do not include confidential information, and remember to target the résumé for the position and highlight specific skills. If you are including a portfolio:

1. Make it easy to find

2. Have an effective home page that prompts more action

3. Include testimonials from colleagues and bosses

4. Show specific examples of work achievements

5. Include a professionally taken head shot

Consider yourself as a brand and manage that brand on a constant basis. Everything you produce to promote yourself needs to be stamped with your brand.

Paul suggests that if you are filing electronically, make sure you have the following formats of résumé:

- Standard Word or PDF version for attaching to e-mails

- Scannable version that can be picked up by employer and recruiter automated tracking software. Keywords are also important in these types of documents.

- One that can be broken into pieces for copying and pasting onto online application forms

As for today's job market trends, Paul sees the résumé as a career marketing document, and while with the advent of more technology the death of the résumé is being predicted, it will likely be a long time before we see the résumé disappearing or being replaced. However, the traditional job search is changing, and with that, the approach and the documents used need to change as well; hence his use of the branded bio and branded skill sheet.

Square Peg Solution — "The personal brand agency dedicated to entrepreneur and executive women and the corporations that market to them." Paul Copcutt can be contacted via e-mail at **paul@squarepegsolution.com**.

CHAPTER 7:

THE POWER OF WORDS

Words evoke emotion, memories, happy thoughts, judgments, and criticisms. This is true on a résumé, where every word you put down will be judged and either discarded or approved within a 15-second window.

Your job is to find the best words in the English language to:

- Represent your skills

- Tell what you can do for a company

- Supply the needs of the position

- Provide proof that you can do all the above

Therefore, use action words whenever possible. Sprinkle keywords throughout to help your résumé be picked up by database search engines.

Write your résumé, then put it away for a bit before you come back to it and take another look. The second time around, you will be able to cut out any unnecessary words and put in more of the ones you want and need to have.

KEYWORDS

There is an untapped gold mine in the use of keywords, if you can only figure out which keywords to use.

Such is the mysterious world of keywords. Employers and companies are increasingly moving to résumé databases as a defense against the thousands of résumés that inundate them daily. This database is a single repository for all résumés that they receive. Electronic résumés are automatically entered, and all paper copies that are faxed, mailed, or dropped off are scanned in using special software.

To have effective use of such a database, the fields are searchable by keywords. This means a recruiter can type in a keyword that matches a job skill they need and have the entire list of people with these skills come up. If you have that same job skill, but your résumé did not contain the one keyword that the recruiter typed in, your name will not come up.

This is the situation in job-hunting today.

So how can we find out what the magic words are? According to an article by Katharine Hansen from **quintcareers.com**, these words are usually nouns. One of the best ways to identify useful keywords is to look at other ads to see what keywords are repeatedly mentioned around a certain job title. Create a list to incorporate into your résumé. If you use one, a search engine will find it. Therefore, use synonyms each subsequent time in order to broaden the amount and types of words that the search engines will find. Once you have found the keywords to use, the next question is, how should these words be used?

In this same article, Hansen says that several years ago it was recommended to front-load your résumé with a laundry list of keywords because, supposedly, database search software would search no more than the first 100 words of your document. This does not seem to apply anymore, if it ever did. However, Hansen still recommends front-loading your résumé.

A keyword summary is advised by some experts, but it is more acceptable to sprinkle the keywords throughout the early part of your document, particularly if you have a summary or professional profile section. In this section, the keywords are in the part of the résumé where you describe your activities and accomplishments. The leap here is to take each keyword you have identified as critical for this job and list an accomplishment that tells how you have used the skill represented by that keyword.

It is impossible to give you a list of keywords guaranteed to be the ones recruiters are looking for. So keep the words mobile in your résumé and use variations on the same word because you do not know what form the recruiter will search for. Examples of this are manager, management, and manage. The recruiter could search for any or all of them. This applies to abbreviations as well; try both CRM and Customer Relationship Manager.

After you have completed the résumé, highlight all the keywords. The current theory is that you should aim for 25 to 35 keywords. If you find you have fewer than this, go back and see if you can add in one or two more.

This is another reason to target your résumé for each job, or at least tweak the keywords in your résumé to each particular job.

PRECISE OR ADAPTIVE WORDS TO USE

These adjectives help describe your skills. Remember the old adage "less is more." You need to be as succinct as you can. Therefore, you need to use the right word instead of a whole sentence of words that say the same thing.

These words paint a precise image that helps you portray who and what you are:

Accurate	Active	Adaptable	Adept
Broad-minded	Competent	Conscientious	Creative
Dependable	Determined	Diplomatic	Discreet
Efficient	Energetic	Enterprising	Enthusiastic
Experienced	Fair	Firm	Genuine
Honest	Innovative	Logical	Loyal
Mature	Methodical	Motivated	Objective
Outgoing	Personable	Pleasant	Positive
Practical	Productive	Reliable	Resourceful
Self-disciplined	Sensitive	Sincere	Successful
Tactful	Trustworthy		

ACTION VERBS TO USE

Use action verbs to describe your functional skills whenever you can.

Accelerated	Activated	Adapted	Administered	Analyzed
Approved	Assisted	Completed	Conceived	Conducted
Controlled	Coordinated	Created	Delegated	Developed
Directed	Eliminated	Established	Evaluated	Expanded
Expedited	Experienced	Expanded	Facilitated	Generated
Implemented	Improved	Increased	Influenced	Initiated
Interpreted	Launched	Led	Lectured	Maintained
Managed	Mastered	Motivated	Organized	Originated
Participated	Performed	Pinpointed	Planned	Prepared
Programmed	Proposed	Proved	Recommended	Reduced
Reinforced	Reintroduced	Removed	Reorganized	Repeated
Reworked	Restored	Revamped	Reviewed	Revised
Set up	Simplified	Solved	Streamlined	Structured
Supervised	Supported	Taught	Trained	Worked

COMMONLY USED ACTION WORDS

The words you use decide the impression you give, and first impressions are all the time you have in the 15-second glance your résumé will get. This is a partial list, as the choices are enormous:

Accomplish	Examine	Adapt	Compile
Administer	Assign	Achieve	Compare
Approach	Serve	Arrange	Catalogue
Analyze	Control	Budget	Relate
Assess	Chair	Apply	Detail
Communicate	Qualify	Calculate	Conceive
Delegate	Employ	Design	Examine
Complete	Correct	Demonstrate	Modify
Edit	Exchange	Determine	Direct

Distribute	Originate	Familiarize	Formulate
Encourage	Review	Draft	Identify
Hire	Identify	Implement	Enlist
Innovate	Institute	Install	Survey
Instruct	Expand	Inspect	Lead
Investigate	Solve	Maintain	Govern
Interview	Review	Moderate	Modify
Monitor	Perform	Introduce	Compile
Present	Originate	Oversee	Persuade
Invent	Preside	Raise	Revise
Process	Represent	Publish	Reccommend

WORDS TO NEVER USE

Words have the power to make or break your résumé. In addition, you need to be able to back up every word you put down on your résumé with facts.

Do not say "experienced" if you cannot prove it.

Scott Bennett, author of *The Elements of Résumé Style* (AMACOM), says that potential employers can see through the constant use of vague phrases and buzzwords used in a résumé. The most successful job seekers list concrete accomplishments instead of vague references to theoretical skills. You need to demonstrate your work ethic and activities with specific examples.

Bennett offers these examples:

Instead of... "Experience working in fast-paced environment."

Try... "Registered 120+ third-shift emergency patients per night."

Instead of... "Excellent written communication skills."

Try... "Wrote jargon-free User Guide for 11,000 users."

Instead of... "Team player with cross-functional awareness."

Try... "Collaborated with clients, A/R, and Sales to increase speed of receivables and prevent interruption of service to clients."

Instead of... "Demonstrated success in analyzing client needs."

Try... "Created and implemented comprehensive needs assessment mechanism to help forecast demand for services and staffing."

Bennett also created a worst-offenders list. Some of the words on this list will surprise you. We use them all the time — particularly on résumés. According to Bennett, you should be careful before putting these empty but current catchwords down. Here is his list of words to be cautious using:

Innovative	Ambitious	Competent
Detail-oriented	Determined	Well-organized
Flexible	Experienced	Hard-working
People person	Efficient	Logical
Independent	Knowledgeable	Professional
Resourceful	Self-motivated	Successful
Goal-oriented	Team player	Reliable
Creative	Aggressive	Motivated

TRANSFERABLE SKILLS LIST

Here is a list of transferable skills that are often used on résumés. The idea here is not to blindly copy these phrases down, but to understand what these types of skills are and create your own list. The only ones that belong on your résumé are the ones that were used for a specific job. The only time you can use these skills without explaining them is on the Qualification Summary. This is only a partial list, and the phrases are broken down into subjects.

Take the time to research other transferable skills if these do not seem to fit.

Leadership

- Self-motivation

- A positive attitude

- Delegate responsibility

- Decision-making integrity

- Negotiate

- Motivate individuals and groups to perform

- Encourage effective teamwork

- Implement plans of action

- Set and follow through on goals

- Identify and manage ethical issues

- Assess and evaluate other people's work

- Manage time through prioritizing and scheduling

- Identify critical issues quickly and accurately

- Organize and plan projects or events

- Train others

Administration

- Interpret rules and regulations

- Present written and oral material

- Ensure that tasks are completed on time

- Time-manage daily workload

- Handle complaints

- Deal with obstacles and crises

- Liaison between different factions

Information Management

- Research information

- Compile and summarize facts, concepts, principles, and data

- Formulate relevant questions and develop ways to supply and clarify answers

- Present facts and ideas clearly, orally, or in writing

- Use various computer programs (list software) and other information technology

- Manage a budget and keep accurate financial records

- Maintain document management system

Creativity

- Solve problems

- Create new processes using science, math, and/or imagination

- Write interesting and clear articles, reports

- Plan and arrange events and activities

- Attend to visual detail

- Assess and evaluate my own work

- Market products to appeal to public

- Create works of art

- Design Web pages

Interpersonal Communications

- Exercise "give and take" to achieve group results

- Understand and work in groups

- Listen actively and attentively

- Delegate tasks and responsibilities

- Coach

- Teach, supervise, and train others

- Conduct in-depth interviews

- Express ideas and thoughts based on facts

- Recognize and mediate

- Speak a foreign language (specify language)

- Use sign language

Personal Development

- Analyze life experiences

- Identify and assess needs, values, strengths, and weaknesses

- Instill self-confidence and self-esteem in others

- Demonstrate flexibility and commitment to change and learning

- Learn the value of hard work and persistence

- Creative stress management

Daily Work

- Organized

- Punctual

- Meeting goals

- Set and meet deadlines

- Attend to details

- Implement decisions

Refer back to the worksheets from Chapter 2. You have a solid list of skills identified now. Some of them will be transferable goals, as they are skills you can move or transfer to a new job.

CHAPTER 8:

THE BASICS OF DESIGN

Now you are ready to start. Until now, you have more or less understood what you have to do, but not quite how to do it yet. That is what comes next.

1. First, collect all the information you are going to need. This includes all previous work experience dates, job titles, addresses, awards, and educational information, including addresses, correct names, and the proper names of the associations you belong to.

2. Decide what format is appropriate; refer back to Chapter 3 if you need to.

3. Set up a blank document on the computer or get out your pen and paper and get started.

Understand that there are several different ways in which people prefer to write. Some like to put down a rough copy, then fix and edit it afterwards; others prefer to write perfect copy the first time. There is no right or wrong way — just different styles. The important thing is to get started. You cannot apply for that dream job without a résumé.

Let us start with the basics of design.

DESIGNING BASICS

A recruiter or HR manager will give your résumé approximately 15 seconds to tell them what they need to know. If it does not do this, they will toss the résumé into the garbage. These professionals receive hundreds of résumés for every job posted. In some cases, they face thousands of résumés for one job. Their job is to work through the pile to find the top 20 or so résumés for a closer look. There is not a magical number here, but you can bet they are looking for the fewest number of "best" résumés.

If they cannot find the information they need in their initial scan, your one chance to make the cut is gone.

Again, there is no one "right" design for a résumé, but there are standards you need to stick to. The only time you would be going against mainstream thinking is if you were applying for a job in a creative field, and even then, being too creative will get your résumé tossed. That does not mean it has to be a cardboard cutout of every other résumé in the pile. Use your common sense.

This is a business representation of who you are. Make it professional looking.

PAGE SETUP

It is standard to use one-inch margins all around your document. Use the normal portrait layout, not landscape layout. Choose the page size for a standard 8 ½" x 11" size sheet of paper.

WHAT FONTS TO USE

Start by making sure you are using a standard font on the computer and not fancy lettering or exaggerated sizes. There are no right fonts and sizes, but there are wrong ones. Stick to standard business-style fonts such as Times New Roman and Courier, or Arial and Helvetica for a more contemporary look. Do not use a smaller font size than 10, as it is too hard on the eyes, and do not use a font larger than 12 for the main body. Size 14 for headings is fine, but do not go any larger. Keep to standard line spacing, ¼" between lines, and do not condense the line spacing.

Use a maximum of two different fonts. One font for the headings and one for the body of the résumé is normal. Anything more than this makes the résumé distracting to read.

This is a business document, not an opportunity to let your creative side free.

The design of your résumé is important. It goes back to that 15-second glance, and, if you are lucky, as long as a 35-second perusal of your résumé. To make it past this first test, you have to make the information easy to read. By following standard formats, you make it easy for recruiters to find the information they want.

NAME AND CONTACT INFORMATION

This section of the résumé tends to be centered at the top of the page. The other common design is to have the heading aligned left. Left aligned is required if you are doing an electronic résumé. The headings, subheadings, and text are aligned to the left for the electronic format.

If you have two sets of contact information, one permanent and one current, split them so the permanent contact information is on the right side and the current information is on the left side. For more information and samples, see the sections on headers and contact information in Chapter 5.

If you prefer, you can put the address information at the bottom of the page, in the footer. This leaves the valuable upper half of the page available for the more important information. A recruiter will not spend time on your name and address at the top, but you do not want to make them hunt for your contact information either.

Your name is one place in a résumé where you can use a larger font, all caps, or even a signature. Your résumé is an ad, and you are the product that it is selling. Make sure the ad promotes the image you want it to.

THE BODY OF THE RÉSUMÉ

If you fold a normal 8 ½″ x 11″ piece of paper from the top down to the bottom and then open it again, the space above the fold is the most important area. It is here that the eyes go first. Given that your résumé will receive so little time, put the most important information in this area. Your résumé is a hierarchy of importance. You would place skills above personal interests and education above publications, unless you are applying for a writing/editing position.

One design style splits the paper in four sections and balances the material from left to right, and from importance, top to bottom. This is not a hard design, but does require an ability to create columns and work in them on your word processing program. This style can be done with tabs and tables, but you need to make sure that you cannot see the dividing lines or outlines. A word of caution on using the space bar to space text out on lines instead of tabs — do not do it. Tabs line up the same every time, whereas the space bar rarely does. Again, this depends on your computer skills.

BOLDING, CAPITALIZING, UNDERLINING, ITALICIZING, AND FIRST LETTER LARGER

These are several methods of adding emphasis to your résumé. These techniques need to be used sparingly. Do not mix them or overuse them. They can be effective for headings and subheadings, but much less so in the body of the text. If overused, they become distracting to the eye, making the résumé hard to read.

Capitalizing what you want to emphasize is effective, particularly for job positions and educational institutions.

Look at the following two options — the first example places the focus on the University, the second places the focus on the degree:

PRINCETON UNIVERSITY, NEW JERSEY
Master of Business Administration

MASTER OF BUSINESS ADMINISTRATION
Backwoods College, Hick Town

The same theory applies to job positions. If you had a great position for a little known company, highlight the job title. If you worked for a well-known company but had a less illustrious job title, highlight the company.

BULLETS

Using bullets is an effective way to make a lot of material clear and easy to understand. Do not use full sentences with bullets; instead, write down just the important point and go on to the next bulleted point.

Use a standard bullet or asterisk symbol. Do not be tempted to use creative symbols as the bullet. If doing an electronic résumé, you will need to use asterisks in place of the bullet, which are not available in text format.

PARAGRAPH STYLE

If you prefer to write in more of a paragraph style, there are hints to make your text more readable.

Keep all paragraphs to fewer than seven lines long. Shorter is better. Divide the information into groups for easy accessibility. Complete the job summary in paragraph form, and then list the specific achievements with bullets.

If you choose paragraph style, you may want to choose full justification. This is where all the lines end at the same place on the right margin. It makes a paragraph-style résumé look more formal. The ragged right-hand margins of left-justified text give a more informal appearance. The lines look neater on full-justified margins.

This is a design choice and is not mandatory.

LINES

Graphic lines are a good way to separate different sections, in particular, the contact information from the body of the résumé. You can change the weight of the line, but do not make it so large as to distract from the information. Decide on one or two different weights and use them throughout the résumé. Consistency is important in creating a professional look.

Lines can be horizontal, vertical, or full-page borders. Horizontal lines between sections allow the reader to look at one section at a time. If done properly, horizontal and vertical lines can add a classy touch to a résumé.

COLOR

Color evokes emotions and helps create an atmosphere. Papers should be neutral or light in color. Brilliant white is the most popular color, followed by slightly off-white shades. Light gray colors have remained popular. If you are gong to use colored paper, keep the colors soft and light, like salmon, light blue, and light green. It will be sure to stand out in the heap of résumés.

A note of caution: Stepping out of the box might get you attention, but it might not be the type of attention you want. Colored paper may get your résumé tossed into the discard pile if the hiring manager does not like résumés on colored paper.

Make sure all the text is in standard black and not with colored headings, unless you are following the rules for creative résumés.

LETTERHEAD

It does not take a graphic designer to create your own letterhead anymore. Many simple programs can make a classy letterhead with a little effort.

If you put your résumé and cover letter together with your letterhead, it makes a sharp, professional impression that will get your application noticed.

GRAPHICS

A traditional résumé is not the place for graphics and photos. I have used the term traditional here because there is also a section on creative résumés in Chapter 3. Chapter 4 focuses on the newer technology résumés and Chapter 14 is dedicated to portfolios. For most people, there should be no graphics, photos, charts and tables, or anything else along this line on your résumé.

This also means that you should not use a pretty design or border around the résumé. Another technique to avoid is the use of a watermark behind the text. These might work for other types of documents, but not your standard business résumé.

PHOTOS

Photographs on résumés are required in some foreign countries when they request a CV. In the United States, they are not normally used, unless you are applying for a position such as an actor, model, or a media position in which your appearance becomes a qualification.

WHITE SPACE

White space refers to the space on a page where there is no text. This space is important for the reader. It is used to draw the eye down the page to what you want seen. Using white space does not confuse the reader with an overabundance of text.

Blocks of text larger than seven lines are considered tiring to the reader. That is why using bullets helps reduce the text and increase the white space.

PAPER

Again, this is a business document. You should print this document on standard white, ivory, or cream office paper. Print on heavy bond, 20 lb. stock and not on a thin, cheap paper. It needs to survive the review process and look good by the time you arrive for your first interview.

Do not send out photocopies of your résumé if you can help it. Original printed copies are best. Print on one side only. Print your résumé on standard letter-size paper only, 8 ½" x 11" in most of North America. If you print on 8 ½″ x 14″ legal paper, the bottom portion of the page might be missed when the résumé is photocopied. Avoid folding your résumé; the fold makes it harder to scan.

If you are applying for a job in another country, be aware that standard paper sizes are different. Find out what size paper is used there. Refer to Chapter 16 for more information on sending applications out to a global market.

Please resist the urge to print on lavender-colored paper and add a drop of perfume for good luck.

CASE STUDY: LOUISE FLETCHER

Louise Fletcher is president of Blue Sky Résumés, a leader in creative résumés and job search strategies. She spent 15 years as an HR executive and had to terminate many employees because the company she worked for was going out of business. In helping some of these people find new work, she discovered a talent for résumé writing, and eventually, Blue Sky Résumés was formed. She is a Certified Professional Résumé Writer (CPRW) and an active member of the Professional Association of Resume Writers (PARW) and the Career Masters Institute.

Her expertise lies in résumé writing, personal branding, and career marketing — both online and offline. Over the years, Louise has seen a move to make career marketing the same as any other marketing — meaning the idea of developing and communicating a personal brand is more popular now. However, she does not think the career-coaching/résumé-writing industry has changed as much as it needs to. She feels that many professionals are being left behind as the Internet revolutionizes the job search process. "We cannot help our clients find jobs if we do not understand all the new opportunities available to them, and the Internet is only going to continue to revolutionize what we do."

Louise says the most important thing to remember about writing an application package today is to differentiate yourself from the other candidates. You need your résumé to answer the employer's concerns and show how you can meet his or her needs. It is important to understand your audience, just like a product marketer. Understand what drives the hiring manager. Once you do that, you can show her or him how and why you are the right person for the job.

CASE STUDY: LOUISE FLETCHER

Louise follows the "less is more" rule on résumés, meaning less content and less fancy formatting. If your résumé has to travel electronically, keep it simple or you risk losing all that formatting. Use plenty of white space and use bolding selectively to draw attention to key sales points.

Louise says that the Web made it very hard for employers to hire, as there were too many résumés to choose from, forcing new systems to be developed to connect employers with the right people. She sees the rise of social networking online as critical. Networking will be as important to the job search as it has always been — it will just happen online as well as offline.

Louise keeps in touch with emerging trends in HR management as a columnist for **Monster.com**. Her articles on job search strategy and résumé writing have been published by numerous Web publications and several of her résumés have been selected for publication in the JISTworks "Expert Résumé" series. She is currently working on a book on creative job search strategies and she maintains the Blue Sky Résumés Blog.

CHAPTER 9:

THE STICKY PARTS

No two résumés are alike, and no two people's stories are alike. Each will have challenges to overcome. For some it will be that they have been out of work for a long time; for others, it will be that they were fired from their last job. Students have unique problems, as do people who are changing careers.

JOB HISTORY PROBLEMS

Looking for a job can be daunting at the best of times. Facing this prospect with less than a sterling work record can be stressful. If you have been out of work for over six months, searching for a job can be horrifying.

There is a tremendous amount of information available on the Internet about the job search issues for those recently laid off. However, what if this is your second or third, or even worse, your fourth layoff in as many years? It can be difficult to put that down on paper and look like a viable candidate for any job.

If you were fired from your last position, there is hope of finding a good job again. However, these types of problems need to be handled properly and not shoved into a corner in hopes that no one will notice blank spots in your work history. Blank spots are red flags for recruiters. If you make it to the interview stage, expect some hard questions.

However, you can reenter the workforce successfully, whether you have been unemployed, self-employed, or just traveling around the world.

In this next section, we take a closer look at some work history problems people experience and ways to fill this area of your résumé without lying or hiding the information.

BEFORE YOU WRITE YOUR RÉSUMÉ

Assess your skills, experience, and competitive advantage for today's market. What are hiring managers looking for in your industry now? What can you offer them? How would an employer benefit from hiring you? With those questions in mind, write down your desirable skills, experience, and training that a hiring manager can easily identify.

Take the time to refresh your skills if they need it. You may need to enroll in courses, volunteer, or practice your skills in some way to bring them back to par for today's marketplace. For example, maybe you are a secretary who stayed home for the last five years to look after the family and are now returning to work. Can you type at 60 wpm? If not, brush up until you can. Not only will it make you marketable again, it will help you regain your confidence.

Staying current with professional activities relevant to your industry will also keep you marketable. This includes participating in community associations, volunteer work, joining professional organizations, attending conferences, and doing consulting, part-time, and temporary or contract work.

WHEN WRITING YOUR RÉSUMÉ

Choose the right format to accent the positive elements of your résumé. Some people do better with a functional résumé over a chronological format; however, it can appear that you are hiding something. The functional résumé should be considered if you have been out of work for many years.

A combination résumé is often the best bet, as it starts with a Qualification Summary before going into reverse chronological order. The summary emphasizes your most relevant skills and qualifications.

- Focus on the positive in your work history. Put the accomplishments and skills learned at the top where they can be immediately identified.

- Do not emphasize dates. Put them down, but do not highlight them with white space.

- Use your cover letter to explain why your work history is the way it is. Did you travel for a year? Did you go back to school? An interview is the best place to explain your history, so do not apologize. State the reasons for your employment history with a positive spin, then explain fully in a face-to-face job interview.

This type of problem does not have to stop you from getting a good opportunity, but you will need to work harder than other job seekers. You might have to accept a lower position or take a cut in pay. There are good opportunities to prove your worth and help you move up from there.

IF YOU ARE RECENTLY LAID OFF

Depending on your industry and the economics of your industry, layoffs are happening on a regular basis. If this is a recent event, besides needing to deal with the depression, anger, sense of betrayal, and fear, you need to take action while your layoff is new. Here is how:

- Update your résumé immediately. Be positive about your current (or recent) position, regardless of your feelings toward the company.

- Collect written reference letters from supervisors and coworkers.

- Do not say you are employed on your updated résumé or put down "to present." Laid off is unemployed.

- Do not mention the layoff. Put that in your cover letter.

- Evaluate your skills against the current employment market. Are you competitive or do you need to upgrade?

- Start job searching while your layoff is recent.

- Focus on your achievements.

- Assess your contributions to the company. Put your feelings aside and think clearly and objectively about what you did while employed. Here are six questions to ask:

  a) What types of challenges did you face?

  b) How did you overcome these same challenges?

  c) How did you contribute to the company's bottom line?

  d) Did you juggle multiple tasks and projects while keeping up a quality performance?

  e) Did you take on work over and above your activities?

  f) What were your measurable accomplishments?

SPOTTY WORK HISTORY

In today's work economy, it is important to appear stable. A spotty work history, if listed incorrectly, will make you appear unstable.

A spotty work history is where you do not have steady, consistent employment at one or two jobs in the same field showing consistent growth. That leaves room for confusion. Even if the loss of the jobs was not your fault, having five or more jobs in a ten-year period can give you the appearance of being a job hopper, someone who maybe is not going to be satisfied, or is always thinking that the next job will be your big break.

If this area is a problem for you:

- Look to the activities that you did while not employed. You might have relevant experience through volunteer activities, the community, or special projects you were involved in. Did you further your education during this time with evening classes, part-time courses, or weekend seminars? You need to dig deeper than the person with a continuous work history, but it is not about why you were not working, but about what you accomplished in this time.

- Search for and list the transferable skills you learned during this time that will apply to a current job.

- Write employment dates so the months are not included if your gaps of unemployment were short.

- Focus on your strengths and accomplishments through a Summary.

- Use an Objective Statement to summarize your goals.

- Demonstrate how you have stayed current with your industry, particularly if returning to work after a long time period.

- Regardless of the reason why you have been out of work, do not make it sound negative or apologize.

- If you were out of work to raise a family, recover from an injury, or even care for another injured person, it is important to put down these years.

Tell what you were doing in a positive way and fill in the gaps. For example:

2002 – 2005 Full-time parent

1997 – 1998 Maternity leave

1996 – 2000 Full-time student

1990 – 2000 Parenting plus volunteer work

JOB HOPPING

For some industries, jobs tend to have a short duration, and this is acceptable. It is not a concern if everyone in the industry has the same type of experience. However, if your industry is not like this, you need to present your experience in a different way.

One of the best ways to change the job-hopper impression is to combine some of the work history. If you were in sales, you could have been a sales rep for one company and then a second company within a couple of months if the first job did not work out. Here you would list your experience as:

Sales Representative, (first company), (second company), 6/2000 – 4/2003

Another example is for contractors. You do not list each individual contract, but instead, group them together under one time-period:

Database Specialist, 4/2004 – 2006

Management Consultant, 3/2001 – present

If you have had many short, unrelated jobs, it will look better if you combine them into one or two entries. For example:

1995 – 1997 Receptionist/Switchboard; Ace Contracting, Magic Mops, Dental Corp.

1997 – 1999 Cocktail Waitress/Bartender; Ali's Pub, Blue Falcon Bar & Grill, Barney's Irish

In situations like this, you need to put down the project accomplishments and highlights. You do not need to put every job on your résumé, but you will need to if you are asked to fill out a job application. This is a signed legal document, and you do not want inconsistencies to come back to you. And if a short-term job is where you acquired an important skill, put it down, regardless of the length of your employment.

A cover letter is a good place to explain any major shortfalls in your work history and gives you an opportunity to put a positive spin on them. It is important to point out the positives and create a résumé that moves forward instead of one that focuses on your history. You cannot change your history; you can only move forward.

CRIMINAL RECORD

It is hard to imagine any blight in your history harder to overcome than a criminal record. However, according to Kim Isaacs in her article, "Criminal Background: How to Address Your Criminal Background," the Bureau of Justice Statistics reports prison releases on the rise, with close to a half a million ex-offenders looking to rejoin the workforce each year.

With the number of obstacles facing those with this type of background, you need to make your résumé as effective as possible. Isaacs recommends the following tips to ensure your résumé is the best it can be:

Do Not Accent Your History —This type of information should only happen during an interview where you can explain more clearly the circumstances surrounding your history. It is important to show that you have the skills and qualifications for the job first. However, if filling out a job application, you must answer "yes" if asked whether you have been arrested before. You can add a note saying you would be happy to explain in an interview.

When the employer asks about your criminal history, explain what happened and that you have learned from the past. Do not dwell on this part of your life; move on to the important skills you have to offer.

Focus on Training/Work Experience — If, while in prison, you participated in training opportunities or worked during this time, put this information in your résumé. Isaacs suggests that you treat the work at the prison as you would any other job, listing the prison, job type, and the work experience on your résumé. This applies to any courses you may have taken while in prison as well, as long as they are relevant to the position. If the education and work experience is from over 10 years ago, you do not need to put them down. Target the résumé the same as everyone else: to focus on the relevant information for the job.

Fill In All the Gaps — If you need to, put in another section on your résumé called Additional Experience in which you would list the prison-related work or training.

OVERQUALIFIED

Finding yourself unemployed and suddenly overqualified for the career field you are in can be devastating. It is important to update your résumé immediately. However, deciding what to put down and how to put it down can be stressful.

Unfortunately, in today's economy, being laid off and being overqualified are common issues, as many career-driven professionals are finding themselves out of work for extended periods. Changing jobs and being forced to reclimb the corporate ladder are also very common.

It would be nice to think that you can wait until the perfect job comes along, but you might have to accept a job lower than you would like, in terms of title, responsibility, and salary. Think of this as the career being your passion and a job is what you have to do until you can make your career move forward.

Taking a job is understandable, but do not stop looking for a better one. It might be necessary to trim down your résumé and minimize your qualifications to move into any job or one that will provide you the chance to move back up again.

Here are some suggestions for managing this situation:

- Continue networking and job-hunting, even after accepting a lower-level position.

- Continually research companies that may provide a chance to move back up the career ladder and provide long-term growth.

- Change jobs as a calculated move to your career growth.

- Consider taking a job that will give you new skills or build on your existing skill set to enhance your marketability and portfolio.

- Create multiple versions of your résumé — one to get a job and one to move you back to the level of job you want.

- Make sure you can appear happy with the salary expectations and respond in kind to this type of questioning from the interviewer.

- Be aggressive in your job search and consider contacting recruiters to help find your perfect job.

- Find out what employers are looking for in your industry and what you need to do to get the much-needed advantage over the competition.

- Pick up any necessary skills to get back into the game.

Some specialists recommend leaving off a qualification that makes you overqualified. This could mean leaving off a PhD and toning down your experience. However, this can make you look dishonest if found out. In addition, if higher-level positions in the company do open up, you will have a hard time explaining your sudden qualifications.

Other specialists recommend forgoing a résumé altogether and trying to get to the hiring manager through networking. If you can get a recommendation through someone already working in the company, this will often open doors for you.

One of the better answers to this problem is not to hide your qualification, but instead explain why you are the best candidate and a perfect fit for the company. In your cover letter, make it clear why you are enthusiastic about the position.

An interview is the best place to explain the issues surrounding accepting a lower job. In an interview, be prepared to answer some questions. Make sure you can:

- Talk comfortably about salary. It is important to be flexible about salary and willing to take a pay cut.

- Sell yourself by stating how your expertise and efficiency will help their bottom line.

- Show that you are up to date on your industry and have great interest in learning new things.

- Show that you are a team player.

- If they are concerned about you leaving for a better position, offer to sign a contract stating you will stay with the company for one to two years.

- Show real enthusiasm for the job and the company.

Like any person applying for a position, make sure you can sell why your experience, skills, and accomplishments make you perfect for the job.

UNDERQUALIFIED

How many times have you looked at a job ad and thought to yourself, "I could do that job," but you did not have the qualifications or the experience? How can you change the employer's perception of your fit for the position in question?

This can be a difficult challenge. Most employers would hire someone who has the right qualifications and experience over someone who does not.

In her article, "Underqualified? Ten Tips to Inspire Employers to Take a Leap of Faith," Kathy Hansen suggests the following:

1. **Use your transferable skills to show how you are the ideal candidate for the position.** If you are a recent graduate, look to your university years to see how you used leadership, teamwork, and communication skills; then show how these skills apply to the job in question.

2. **Use unpaid experience and school experience to fill out your employment experience in the required field.** Remember, experience is valuable regardless of where it was learned.

3. **In a résumé where your work history is not a strong selling point, consider a combination format where you can highlight your outstanding skills and achievements.** This deemphasizes your work history.

4. **Employment ads are an employer's wish list.** But you do need to have some of the required qualifications before applying for the job.

5. **Show that you are eager to gain more training and eager to learn.** If a special license is required, say that you are willing to do the work to achieve this standing. This could put you into the "underqualified but trainable" category, and will often give you a leg up on the competition.

6. **Consider supplying a career portfolio with your résumé.** These

are samples of your best work and can make the difference in an interview with an interviewer who is not convinced of your qualifications.

7. **Consider volunteer work on a trial basis for little to no money.** This also shows enthusiasm and willingness to do what is required. Hansen also suggests that, instead of a time period, ask to work on a typical project on an unpaid basis to show you can do the job.

The full article can be read at **http://www.quintcareers.com/underquali-fied-unqualified_job-seeker.html.**

If you are not successful in your job application, consider taking some training to supply a missing skill that will help when the next opportunity comes around. Even if your training is not complete, taking it shows initiative and enthusiasm.

ENTRY LEVEL

There are many ads for entry-level positions, which are a great way to start your career path right out of school.

With this type of résumé, it is important to put down all your various work experiences on your résumé. Make sure to include internships, student work experience, student work exchange, and part-time and full-time summer jobs. All experience is valuable and has something to offer a new employer.

This is the type of résumé in which you can show off your grades from college. Entry-level positions are often handed out to students with the best grades and not the most experience. These grades show diligence, intelligence, and a hardworking attitude.

Make sure your résumé is perfect. Nothing shows a lack of professionalism more than a résumé riddled with mistakes. Take the time and effort to project the right image as you step out onto your career path.

RELOCATION AND RÉSUMÉS

If all things were equal, employers would prefer to hire locally versus someone from another town, state, or country. It is easier to schedule interviews, and there are no cost questions arising over relocation. That does not change the fact that, according to data from **Monster.com**, half of all job seekers are interested in relocating for the right opportunity.

If you are planning to move or are interested in relocation, here are some suggestions to help your résumé attract the right attention:

At some career sites, like **Monster.com**, there is an option you can click such as, "I am willing to relocate." Employers who are searching résumés have the option of including those résumés from people who both reside in or are willing to work in their selected location. It helps to make sure your name comes up in their search results.

If you are targeting a specific region, add that information to your career objective: "Searching for a position in the Seattle area," or if you are looking for a region, consider "Open to relocating in the Southwest." If you have plans in place, put down "Relocating to Denver in September 2008."

Use your cover letter to explain your situation:

- "Please note that I will be relocating to Reno in December 2008. This position offers the opportunity and challenge I enjoy. I would welcome a chance to discuss the opportunity with you."

- "At this stage in my career, I am open to relocating for the right opportunity."

As one of the drawbacks of being out of town is your availability for interviews, make sure you plan to be in that area for a specific period to conduct interviews. You can mention in a cover letter that you are available for a certain time or that you will be able to travel to this location for interviews. It is also possible to suggest an initial phone interview with a second one face to face.

Some companies who recruit aggressively offer a package that covers all relocation costs, spousal relocation costs, and may even help in finding a new home. For the rest of the job seekers, it might help if you offer to pay relocation costs yourself. It can be a powerful selling point: "I will be relocating to Salt Lake City in October at my own expense."

Given the edge that a local candidate may have for a coveted position, it is easy to understand why some people try to get an edge in by fudging their address. However, if your job is in one city and your address is in another, the hiring manager might either get confused or feel that you are hiding something. Consider if they call to set up a job interview for the next morning, but you are too far away to make it in time.

It is better to be honest about where you are living and the reasons why you are interested in making this move.

HOW TO HANDLE HAVING HAD ONLY ONE EMPLOYER

To write a dynamic résumé when you have had only one employer can be difficult to achieve. It used to be that staying with a company for thirty years was a strong sign of job security and loyalty. Today, however, it is likely to get you questioned as to why you have not moved on to a better opportunity.

You need to stop any hiring manager's doubts immediately. Here are some suggestions as to how to achieve this:

1. If your job titles are not a good indicator, then use your job descriptions. The first step is to show how far you have come. Show where you started in this company and each step you took to where you are now. State your job titles to show your career advancement.

2. List dates if your jobs have changed consistently, showing growth. If, however, you have been at the same position for the last four to five years, then do not emphasize dates. This situation highlights and questions your potential to be promoted.

3. Show how versatile your skills are and emphasize how you adapted to different responsibilities, managers, departments, teams, and coworkers. Show how your skills moved to new jobs, all the while growing and developing. If you were not promoted or if your job did not change over the years, then it is even more important to highlight the diversity of your skills.

4. Remember to use numbers. List facts and figures about the money you saved, the budget you handled, the sales you increased, and the staff you managed.

5. Make the information clear. Use subheadings to break out special training, skills, results, and achievements. If you have a lengthy list of bullets, this is a good way to make them stand out.

6. If you have only one job and that one has been short, then it is important to put down all experience, including paid and unpaid, student work exchanges, co-op work, and internship experience.

7. Any experience outside of the one job is valuable in that it shows you are comfortable in a variety of different settings.

SALARY ISSUES

Most companies will have an established salary scale or budget for any position within the company. Although they will know the figures prior to posting a position, these budgets can be flexible, depending on what the candidates have to offer. Often candidates will have skills that will benefit the company but may be outside of the established duties of the posted position. In other companies, the budget is fixed. It is in these cases that a request for salary requirements and/or salary history is common. They are stating that salary is a major factor.

SALARY EXPECTATION

How do you address the prospective employer's request to respond with salary expectations? There are several thoughts on this, such as:

- Ignore the request and possibly get disqualified at the beginning.

- List a salary and possibly be excluded as too high.

- Put down that your salary is negotiable.

- Provide the salary figure you want, but only after you have thoroughly researched salaries for similar jobs. Make sure that the lowest end of the range is the minimum you are prepared to work for, with the understanding you have of all the responsibilities and duties involved.

Salary discussions are best done in a job interview. This can be stated in your cover letter. If you choose to put down a salary range, then also put this in the cover letter. Salary figures do not belong on your résumé.

There are several possible reasons companies ask for salary expectations:

1. They are looking to reduce the number of applicants based on salary expectations.

2. They are fishing to see what skills can be bought at what price.

3. The company is trying to figure out whether they can afford you.

4. The company could be trying to find out whether you are a lower-level employee than they want to hire.

5. The company wants to see whether you can follow directions.

SALARY HISTORY

There are a few reasons why an employer would want to know your previous salary history:

- To gain an advantage at the bargaining table

- To weed out candidates who are too high

- To weed out candidates who are too low

For a position with a budget of $50,000 and a candidate used to making $75,000, they will assume the candidate will not be interested in that large of a wage drop and the candidate will be dropped from consideration. If the candidate has a very low salary history, the hiring manager may think they are not capable of the duties and requirements of this position. If the candidate has a low salary history, then the hiring manager may see a good chance to hire someone who will be happy to negotiate their salary and be hired on budget. The manager may even see an opportunity to negotiate and save costs by coming in under budget.

This can make it hard to find the "right" figures to aim for. These type of employers generally have a fixed idea of what they are looking for, what salary this person should have come from, and what they should be doing for that salary. That can make it difficult, as they are looking more to your history than to your future with them.

For this type of document, it is best to create a separate document that is similar to the type of layout and format of both your cover letter and résumé or CV. Try to use the same letterhead, font, format, and stationery whenever possible. Write it in reverse chronological format, beginning with your most recent position.

Here is a sample layout:

Your title
Company name
Dates employed
Salary — List either an annual salary, or alternately, list the starting
salary and then on the next line the ending salary. This shows your
promotions and advancements.

Examples would look like this:

SALARY HISTORY

Option 1: Office Manager
123 Industries, Seattle, WA
July 2001 – April 2007
Annual Salary: $48,000

Option 2: Office Manager
123 Industries, Seattle, WA
July 2001 – April 2007
Beginning Salary: $28,000, plus insurance
Ending Salary: $48,000, plus insurance, 401(k) and daycare expenses

Make sure you include any other compensation beside the wage. As in
the example above, list any insurance benefits, 401(k), commissions,
daycare expenses, and bonus packages. List any individual items that add
to your employment.

Do you have to provide this salary history? If this is a job you really want
and the ad states, "only submissions that include salary history will be
considered," or something along those lines, then yes, you need to provide
it. If the wording is not quite so closed, then you can make the manager
aware that the information will be supplied upon request; something like,
"Salary history will be provided during an interview."

CHAPTER 10:

SPECIALTY RÉSUMÉS

One résumé is not meant to be for every job. Some situations are so specialized that they need to be handled with extra care. With that in mind, here are specific considerations for each of the following:

- The executive résumé

- The career change résumé

- The self-employed résumé

- The military career résumé

- The IT résumé

THE EXECUTIVE RÉSUMÉ

An executive or senior professional must stand out in today's job market. Your résumé must immediately show the bottom line as to what you bring to the company. Executive searches are extremely selective, and your résumé must sell your best qualifications quickly and clearly or you will lose out to another candidate whose résumé speaks clearer. Remember, executives are only hired when there is a real need. They will be reviewing applicants with these thoughts in mind:

- Can you solve their financial problems?

- Will you triple their annual sales?

- Can you transform their failing marketing program?

As for any résumé, try to follow these basic guidelines for the best results.

1. Give employers what they want — This is done by matching your skills to their needs. Put in an executive summary that shows the value you will bring to a company.

2. Focus the résumé to the position.

3. Prove that you can do what you say you can do. State your accomplishments to show what you have done — managed large budgets, trained multiple staff, increased annual sales, or any other way that you added something to your previous employers.

4. Describe the challenge and your solution and then show how you did what you said you did.

5. Have the layout, design, and content of your résumé show what a professional you are.

Several major points to remember when putting together this résumé:

•   The most important element is your value proposition. The recruiter or hiring manager wants to know what ability you have that will solve their business problems, meet their goals, and produce their desired results. Make sure that what you state here is supported with proof from your career.

•   An executive résumé has to state that you understand the needs of the employer and that you can meet them.

•   This profile is the result of your career. List reports, dollar figures, authority you had, sales margins improved, and anything else that demonstrates your accomplishments.

- Explain the challenges, your actions, the results, and that you can do it again.

- Use strong but appropriate words to give more impact to your résumé.

- Let the résumé be the length it needs to be. A three- to five-page résumé is normal for senior executive résumés.

- Only put in content that supports your proposition and give strong emphasis to the most relevant accomplishments. If a skill or job is not applicable, do not put it in.

- Do not put down personal information. Do not list your religious affiliations, family status, or hobbies. Do list any professional associations, board memberships, or related volunteer work.

Following are two examples of executive résumés. The first is an executive résumé of Roger Caldwell. It is reprinted with permission from Barbara Safani of **CareerSolvers.com**. The second is a VP résumé of Peter M. Taylor. It is reprinted with permission from Susan Guarmeri of **www. assessmentgoddess.com**.

EXAMPLE OF AN EXECUTIVE RÉSUMÉ

ROGER CALDWELL   10 Burns Street   Forest Hills, NY 11375
                                      H: 718-268-0989   C: 646-826-1818
                                                     rcaldwell@gmail.com

STRATEGIC PROJECT MANAGEMENT EXECUTIVE

Enterprise Level Telecommunications Projects   Multi-Site/Multi-Disciplinary
                             Team Management
   M.S. Telecommunications   Certified PMP   Microsoft Project Orange Belt
                               Certification

EXECUTIVE PROFILE

Take-charge project management executive with over 15 years' experience orchestrating high visibility projects for best-in-class telecommunication leaders. Adept at building teams, increasing accountability, creating structure, standardizing procedures, and resolving conflict to deliver multimillion-dollar initiatives on-time and on-budget.

SUMMARY OF QUALIFICATIONS

Project Management	*Human Capital Management*	*Sales & Compliance*
Project Planning & Reporting	Cross-Functional Teambuilding	Legal/Regulatory Compliance
Feasibility Analysis	Conflict Resolution	Budgeting/Cost Reduction
Project Modeling	Virtual Conference Mediation	Service Order & Billing
Service Evaluation	Staff Training/Mentoring	Technical Sales Presentations

PROFESSIONAL EXPERIENCE

TELCOM, New York, NY   **2000 to Present**
Senior Staff Consultant/Project Manager, Network Services/Product Deployment (2004 to Present)
Project- manage service launch and public offering of premier advanced optical service; ensure operational readiness and manage $100M in business. Liaise with 30-50 member cross-functional, geographically dispersed teams including Wholesale, Legal & Regulatory, Regional Operations Centers, and Network Engineering & Planning.
Cost Savings
- **Completed eight optical service launches on time and saved previous overrun costs of $62M** by improving project documentation and diversifying team resources.
- **Eliminated close to $700K in service order rework and contract penalties** by implementing pre-launch performance and equipment testing initiative.
- **Slashed service overview training expenses by $250K** by utilizing existing in-house training products and hosting virtual technology seminar for 30 team members.

Business Process Improvement
- **Identified and resolved close to 100 servicing issues annually** by creating action plan register and holding team members accountable for resolution.
- **Improved functional launch team's credibility and efficiency exponentially** by expanding team size from eight to 25, tracking action items and critical issues more judiciously, and assigning subject matter experts to specific projects to enhance product delivery.
- **Decreased post-launch support needs by 75%** by creating reporting tool for senior management that communicated deployment issues, improved quality, and kept team on track for on-time delivery.

Leadership Initiatives
- **Significantly reduced team conflict and broke down departmental silos** by restructuring meeting formats, increasing communication vehicles, documenting service gaps and mediating disagreements.
- **Nominated for Verizon Excellence Award and rated in top 10%** among peer group as an emerging talent in the organization.
- **Certified IT Project Management Adjunct Professor,** Boston University.

EXAMPLE OF AN EXECUTIVE RÉSUMÉ

ROGER CALDWELL   Page Two

Senior Project Manager, Enterprise Solutions Group (2000 to 2004) – *Supported Telcom's new products and broadband services. Interfaced with product marketing, technical services, and operations planning teams to ensure that external customer service trial was implemented and evaluated properly. Supported $50M in contracts annually.*
Business Development

- **Contributed to $35M in new business** by introducing proposal based templates, labor pricing tools, and project implementation plans that marketed value add of service and secured customer buy-in.
- **Instrumental in securing $32M increase in new business with Bank of New York, Commerce Bank, and the Federal Government;** created project manager policies and procedures that improved post-launch customer service and accelerated opportunities to secure additional business.
- **Managed and performed proposal support for over 100 large national RFPs.**

Leadership & Process Reengineering

- **Spearheaded implementation team concept** to improve delivery for $66M flagship IP-VPN service.
- **Created vision for and managed 30-person two-year process improvement team** resulting in development of document repository, post launch evaluation study, and standard project management guidelines for critical network creation activities that enhanced quality, eliminated duplication of work, and improved ability to deliver projects ahead of schedule and under budget.

NATIONAL TEL, New York, NY   1999 to 2000
Network Systems Engineer, Data Solutions Group - *Provided pre-sales design support for IP and network integration services. Worked closely with corporate account manager and customer. Offered complex technical response and solutions to contracts valued up to $50M.*

- **Won $5M bid** to provide Deutsche Bank's global voice mail system.

TEL TECHNOLOGIES, New York, NY   1998 to 1999
Design Specialist, Business Communication Systems - *Led teams responsible for deployment of 2,500 seat banking call center and various PBX installations in NYC. Provided pre-sales design support and customer demonstrations for Tel's Definity PBX, Intuity Voice mail and Conversant products.*

NEW YORK TEL, New York, NY   1989 to 1998
Network Operations - *Promoted through a series of increasingly responsible network operations positions involving development, implementation, and management of new carrier class telecommunication services.*

- **Provisioned the company's first DS3 Frame Relay Line and first ATM network** representing $32M in business: grew network 100% and completed project within aggressive 15-month deadline.
- **Deployed time-critical eight-month fiber optic transmission network surveillance center** that became the primary center for fiber optics surveillance in New York State.
- **Trained 35 technicians and managers**; negotiated with field managers to provide free labor support.

EDUCATION

M.S., Telecommunications, Pace University, New York, NY
B.S., Electrical Engineering, State University of New York at Albany, Albany, NY

TECHNOLOGY

Service implementation for top tier NGADM manufacturers, Lucent, Nortel, Fujitsu, Cisco, & Ciena; VoIP systems including Lucent Centrex IP & Cisco, IP-VPN service; ATM, SONET, Frame relay and IP network; Lucent Definity PBX, Intuity Voice Mail and Conversant products; equipment room design for HVAC & power

EXAMPLE OF A VP RÉSUMÉ

PETER M. TAYLOR

7273 Appleview Drive
715-355-5555 Wausau, WI 54401
petertaylor@e-mail.com

Home:

VICE PRESIDENT / DIRECTOR OF HUMAN RESOURCES

Training & Development • Organizational Development • Talent Development

Senior Human Resources Generalist and OD Director recognized for catalyzing positive change in individuals and business units while containing costs. Aligned HR as strategic business partner and built continuous-learning environments. High-profile innovator across HR functions, including enterprise-wide e-learning and staff retention. Solid background in HR administration, employee relations, compensation, benefits, performance management, training, and regulatory compliance (ADA, OSHA, FLSA, ERISA, AA/EEO, FMLA).

VALUE OFFERED

Strategic Planning & SOPs Initiatives	Human Resources Administration	E-Learning
Training & Curriculum Design Planning	Needs Assessment / Gap Analysis	Succession
Staff Retention Initiatives Management	Employee & Management Development	Change
Team Building & Motivation Learning	Performance Management & Testing	Adult
Enterprise Learning Strategies literate	Employee & Labor Relations	PC and MAC

PROFESSIONAL EXPERIENCE

WISCONSIN STATE POLICE (WSP), Madison, WI
1981 to Present

Lead law-enforcement agency with 4400 employees and five unions. Diversified mission of police services, boat and aviation patrol, investigation, scientific and support services, homeland security, and training.

Commanding Officer (Major), Identification and Information Technology – **June 2006 to Present**

Commanding Officer (Major), Human Resources Section – **October 2004 to June 2006**

Promoted through progressive HR and senior-management positions as strategic change agent. Oversaw budgets of $20 million to $50 million with direct and indirect supervision of up to 300 personnel.

- **Change Management:** Transformed HR from administrative role to strategic business partner, driving key performance initiatives to meet emerging demands of post-9ll and intelligence-led policing environment.
  - Retooled Training Bureau to deliver best-practices law-enforcement training to local and county police officers (outside WSP). Now revenue-generating program ($15,000 profit from first class held).
  - Expanded college-level CEU accreditation across all training and development programs.
  - Expanded firearms training across entire continuum of force (psychological, physical, and self-defense).
  - Led paradigm shift for medical services from reactive to proactive health and wellness training.
- **HR Management:** Administered $20 million budget annually for diverse HR functions: health and welfare benefits, employee and labor relations, performance management, training and development, and OD. Captured $5 million in cost avoidance by reducing enlisted sick leave by more than 50%.
- **HR Web Site:** Spearheaded development of complex (340 pages and 700 links) HR web site that grew into critical information-sharing and e-learning tool. Now second-most-visited site in WSP web site.
- **Training and Development:** Innovated 10 new professional-development training programs using in-house subject-matter-experts that saved $50,000 over six months. Oversaw development of confidential, highly sensitive random drug-testing program for troopers, which won support from union leadership.
- **Team-building Leadership:** Designed and co-delivered teambuilding training for 125 staff using adult learning principles (group work and hands-on exercises) that raised group morale and synergy scores.
- **Leadership Training:** Built foundation for careerpathing and succession planning through keynote addresses to 300 new supervisors over two years on strategic thinking, ethics, and professional development.
- **IT Leadership:** Re-vitalized and led cost-saving WAN migration saving $1.24 million. Upgraded enterprise-wide emergency systems and field-response teams, and improved network security.

EXAMPLE OF A VP RÉSUMÉ

PETER M. TAYLOR
Page 2

Home: 715-355-5555 ▪ petertaylor@e-mail.com

PROFESSIONAL EXPERIENCE

Chief (Captain), Organizational Development Bureau - November 2003 to October 2004

Tapped to head up newly formed bureau and challenged with enhancing organizational development.

- **OD Leadership:** Championed and established OD Bureau, with 12 staff and fully operational systems in three months. Introduced strategic planning and SOPs for change initiatives involving promotions process and testing, academic partnerships, organizational re-structuring, e-learning, and risk management.
- **Strategic Partnerships:** Grew academic-institution partnerships and encouraged employees' professional development through on-site education fairs, supervisory coaching, and motivational mentoring. Result: number of Bachelor's Degree holders increased by 35%, although not required for retaining job.
- **Risk Management:** Led cross-departmental risk-management assessment of 200 policies and SOPs. Focused training on mission-critical topics, and launched e-learning pilot project to quickly disseminate training.
- **Project Management:** Administered multi-site promotional testing for 1500 employees. Assessed policies, conducted focus groups, and collaborated with union officials to conclude all testing within one month.

Chief (Captain), Human Resources Bureau - December 2001 to November 2003

Assistant Chief (Lieutenant), Human Resources Bureau - December 2000 to December 2001

Directed HR operations: hiring, labor relations, promotions, transfers, employee benefits, and $200 million payroll for 4200 civilian and non-civilian (union) employees. Supervised 60 HR generalists and specialists.

- **HR Leadership:** Led committee (including union leaders) that conducted broad staffing study, developing up-to-date staffing goals, resource-allocation plans, and budgets for submittal to state legislature.
- **Change Management:** Initiated re-instatement of 250 civilian promotions, held up for two years due to budgetary concerns, after careful fiscal analysis and operations review showed minimal financial impact.
- **Performance Assessment:** Played key role in assessment, development, training, and roll-out of new performance evaluation report to 3,000 management and supervisory personnel.

Assistant Chief (Lieutenant), State Regulatory Bureau - April to December 2000

Promoted to Bureau Chief to devise and implement change management. Supervised staff of 30.

- **Strategic Re-structuring and Performance:** Consolidated units for cost efficiency, and contributed to committee that designed, implemented, and trained on new performance evaluation system.
- **Continuous Improvement:** Revised and upgraded investigation and firearms-safety handbooks, updated private-detective applications, and improved customer service by reducing service backlogs.

Administrator, Special and Technical Services - 1995 to 2000

Oversaw specialized investigative support unit, supervising team of five. Participated in cutting-edge strategic projects, including forensic-laboratory accreditation, terrorism exercises, and alternate-workweek program.

PREVIOUS CAREER HISTORY: Promoted from Trooper to Detective, Investigations.

EDUCATION & LEADERSHIP

MS, Dynamics of Organizations (with Honors) - University of Wisconsin, Madison, WI - 2001
BS, Business Administration (HR major) - University of Iowa, Iowa City, IA - 1991
Certificate in Criminal Justice (Class Valedictorian) - Wisconsin State Police Academy, Madison, WI

Professional Development: University of Wisconsin Management Training Initiative - 2000
State Police Pension Board Member - appointed June 2006

THE CAREER CHANGE RÉSUMÉ

Finding a job in today's market is hard enough when you are staying in your career, but when you are looking to change careers, it can be more difficult.

When looking to change careers you need to present your skills differently. You should focus on the transferable skills that relate to the current career objective — the skills you learned in your previous career that will be of benefit in your newly chosen career.

A career change résumé has to portray several things to the recruiter or hiring manager:

- That the skills you learned in your past jobs will transfer to the one you are applying for

- That your accomplishments complement the industry and position you want to change to

- That you can do jobs different from your current employment

This type of résumé is one that requires a career objective. This is where you get to tell a prospective employer what skills, strengths, and accomplishments you think are transferable.

In many circumstances, when changing careers, you do not have any real experience in this field required to make a strong first impression. This is why you need to present your transferable skills to show a prospective employer what skills you can bring to the organization.

These skills can be from any area, including past work experience, volunteer work, education settings, community associations, and even from participating in hobbies.

A way to understand transferable skills is to divide them into several areas.

Information Skills: This includes planning, researching, policy development, record keeping, information management, designing, programming, calculating, editing, writing, classifying, and compiling information.

People Skills: This group includes all the skills associated with the people you interact with on a daily basis, such as customers, vendors, coworkers, bosses, teams, groups, students, and anyone else you cross paths with. These skills also include the type of interaction, such as negotiating, helping, counseling, interviewing, and training.

General Skills: These are the more commonly understood skills, such as software, instruments, vehicles, food, even skills with plants and animals.

Remember to highlight the skills that are of most value to the new position. Put down everything relevant and leave off the rest. Chapter 7 provides more information on this subject, as well as examples of different transferable skills.

Make sure you address the career-change issue in the cover letter. Do not make excuses. Instead, briefly describe what sent you to the new field and what skills you are bringing with you.

THE SELF-EMPLOYED RÉSUMÉ

Self-employed people have a bigger challenge when it comes to writing a résumé that will help them return to the workforce. However, they also have more initiative and problem-solving abilities than many of those in the workforce. These people often do not understand the range of work skills they have gained though running their own businesses. They could have been consultants, daycare owners, human resource specialists, residential builders, landscapers, and even freelance writers. In each of these cases, skills learned will further your career goals.

To understand these types of skills, you have to do some self-evaluation. This is no different from what any other person who is writing a résumé has to do, except these others may already have a handy job description to draw from.

Highlight those attributes that are perfect for the potential job and focus your résumé to respond to the requirements of the job ad.

The trick for any résumé is to maximize what you can do. If you have little work experience and plenty of solid education, make that the focus. Remember to highlight any courses you may have taken before or during the years you were running your business. If you have been self-employed for many years, you need to list this in such a way that your value can be immediately seen. Fill out the worksheets below. Once you start assessing your skills, it is easier to see your worth. This will boost your self-confidence, and that in turn will help you word these skills in a more dynamic way to make them pop. Do not forget to include your past education and job experiences.

SELF-EMPLOYMENT WORKSHEET

Education

List any prior education and training that you have completed; make sure to include seminars, part-time, and full-time classes.

_____

_____

Experience

Here, list the job duties that you have performed while running your own business. Remember the areas that are often forgotten, like marketing, advertising, copywriting (brochures, pamphlets, menus), hiring/training/scheduling if you had staff, customer service, expansion planning, overseeing inventory control, ordering, accounting, sales, product satisfaction, and even logistics.

_____

_____

Here is where you need to get more specific. Add in numbers. How many staff were you working with? What size budget did you manage?

_____

_____

What about the intangible skills you have developed? List the life skills that are hard to categorize but that people who have run their own business will understand

---

SELF-EMPLOYMENT WORKSHEET

completely. Some suggestions to consider here are patient, motivator, goal-oriented, and problem solver.

_____

_____

Now let us look at an example. Here is what most self-employed people write:

> 1994 – 2002 Owner/Operator — secretarial service business
>
> 1998 – 2000 Owner/Operator — construction company building residential houses
>
> 1996 – 2004 Self-employed — freelance writer

In none of the above cases does the information say anything about what you accomplished or what you can bring to a new company.

Instead, get specific, use bullets, list the company name, if appropriate, and your accomplishments.

Systems Consultant

Systems Inc., September 2004 – present

- Analyze clients' computer system needs to improve business and manufacturing functions

- Increase the efficiency of existing systems by introducing new software and hardware

- Present and defend recommendations to board

Here is another example with a different look. This example is listed by skill and not by job title.

Personnel Management

Personnel International 1993 – 2003

- Recruited/trained over 25 staff, including assistant managers, customer service, and administrative staff filling full-time and part-time positions.

- Hired, trained, and supervised a staff of eight, with the responsibility of quarterly and annual performance evaluations and benefits management.

- Managed operations including customer service, accounting, auditing, inventory control, and purchasing for a sales department of $1 million annually.

Consider your application from a prospective employer's position. They need to know that, if they hire you and invest their time and money into training you, you will be there in a year's time. Putting self-employed on a résumé may raise questions with a potential employer, such as:

- Were you self-employed because you were in between jobs?

- Did you want to start your own business instead of working for a company?

- Are you working as a freelancer or consultant now?

- If so, will you continue to do this in the future?

- If yes, how will that conflict with this position?

- What is your long-term goal with your business?

There are some negative concerns that may come up. If you anticipate these concerns, you can address them up front in your cover letter. Some of these may include:

- That you failed to support even yourself and now are looking for someone else to support you. How does this add to the profit of the company?

- That you are a poor independent planner and worker.

- That you are still running your own business and will be taking advantage of company connections to further your own agenda.

- That you will not take direction well.

- That you want a job to gain future clients for your own business or to learn trade secrets for your own purposes.

Perhaps you chose self-employment because of the flexibility it allows when handling extraneous circumstances. Now that those circumstances have been handled, you wish to return to where your regular employment stopped. This type of situation can empower you, making you appear to be an innovator, problem solver, and someone who can take control.

Remember, if you pick up only an occasional freelance project, you do not need to list this on your résumé. If you worked for a period longer than three months, you do need to put it down. However, if you have major gaps in your employment history and you did freelance work during this time, you need to put down as much of it as you can to fill the holes.

Make sure your cover letter addresses any anticipated concerns of the recruiter or hiring manager. Refer to anything that may raise questions up front. Do not apologize for being self-employed. Do explain how being self-employed fits into your professional goals.

If you are applying for full-time work, and yet will be keeping the business, explain how you will balance these two roles in the future.

Make sure your résumé and cover letter are professional and present you as a viable candidate for the job. Focus on the positive experiences that being self-employed has given you, the skills you have developed, and make sure the potential employer understands how this will benefit the company if you are hired.

SELF-EMPLOYED AND PLANNING TO STAY THAT WAY

If you are self-employed and want to stay that way, it is important to update your résumé on a regular basis. Potential clients and customers will need to know about your accomplishments and past experience. Showing them a current, comprehensive résumé will show your professionalism and your skills.

Follow the same information for those self-employed people wanting to return to the workforce to maximize your strengths and show your accomplishments. Having a dynamic résumé available to potential clients is a great way to further your business goals.

THE MILITARY CAREER RÉSUMÉ

A military career offers a wealth of experience that can be translated into private-sector occupations. Many résumé experts specialize in military career transition résumés. If you need to complete this type of résumé, some elements require special attention.

The trick is to translate military language into résumé language. This is particularly important when considering job titles, as the military job titles are often difficult to understand for relevance in today's job economy. In her book, *Résumés for Dummies*, Joyce Lain Kennedy discusses the issue at length. Here are a few of her examples:

- If you worked in the kitchens as a mess cook, this translates into food service specialist experience.

- If you were a Quartermaster, you were a supply clerk.

- If you were a platoon sergeant, use the title "unit supervisor" instead.

- Rather than trying to explain what a military arms dispersal specialist does, explain that you facilitated the availability of supplies.

If you have trouble trying to translate your military experience into civilian language, check out the MOS Decoder at **Military.com**. This is a free, online military-to-civilian skills identifier.

You also need to identify your strongest transferable skills that you can use to show how you make an ideal employee for any company. With this list in hand, the next step is to tailor your résumé to the job in question. When writing down your experience, treat the military as a corporation and list it as any other person would list their job experiences. Refer to each position you had. Avoid all military jargon and acronyms when writing the résumé and when speaking during a job interview.

It can help ease the transition to the private sector if you join a professional association in your field of choice. Networking is an excellent way to make business contacts to further your professional goals. Search for businesses that would suit your discipline and target agencies or companies that require security clearances, if you have one.

Another possibility is to use a search firm that specializes in placing military personnel who are transitioning into private-sector careers. These firms usually have a network of potential companies that might be in need of your skills.

Finding your niche in the private sector is easier if you can remain flexible about the geographic location of your next job. This also allows the potential to target companies all across the United States.

It is important to remember that military training helps people learn the skills, discipline, and work ethic that are welcome in any private sector career.

THE IT RÉSUMÉ

IT résumés are traditionally skill-based and are therefore ideal for a functional résumé format, as this highlights your skills and experiences.

Start with a summary explaining your skills so that the relevant information is instantly available to recruiters. Highlight your accomplishments and mention your responsibilities. This will also engage the reader and encourage him or her to continue on to the rest of the résumé. Do not forget to mention areas that are traditionally lacking in IT personnel. This includes skills like leadership, management, teamwork, interpersonal skills, and especially any communication skills. The "geek" image needs to be replaced with a cooperative, communicative, and easy-to-get-along-with image.

- Emphasize your skills with short sentences:

  ○ Programmer with eight years' experience with Oracle

  ○ Ten projects in seven years in C++, HTML, and PYTHON

- Make sure to write the terminology for your industry correctly and proofread your résumé with an eye out for jargon mistakes.

- Keep your information short and concise. Use bullet points to present a good deal of information in a short time. Most IT specialists have several certifications — MCSE or MCDBA, for example. List them under a separate heading so they are set off and easy to see.

- Keep your résumé professional and honest.

If you have a large portfolio and are wondering about putting this online, see Chapter 14 on portfolios for more information.

The following is a sample of a Technology Résumé: by Jane Simmons. It was provided by Barbara Safani of **careersolvers.com**.

EXAMPLE OF A TECHNOLOGY RÉSUMÉ

JANE SIMMONS
200 West 45th Street, 10G • New York, NY 10019 • H: 212-555-5667 • M: 646-682-2387 •
Jane_simmons@gmail.com

TECHNOLOGY BUSINESS STRATEGIST • IT Enterprise Roll-Outs • Financial Consolidation Systems • Sarbanes Oxley Implementation • Post Merger Integrations • Risk Assessment and Mitigation • International Business/Alliance Development

Over 15 years' experience managing technology needs for international client base with ten of those years working directly with Fortune 500 firms. Expertise implementing financial consolidation systems in conjunction with change management initiatives, corporate acquisitions, and departmental start ups. Proven ability to deliver solutions that reduce operating expenses by millions of dollars, improve departmental efficiencies exponentially, and significantly diminish firm's exposure to risk. Big picture thinker with knack for explaining technical information in a way that inspires user confidence and cross-functional collaboration.

AREAS OF EXPERTISE

Technology Driven Transformation
- Corporate, business unit, & enterprise technology
- Competitive & impact analysis of technology products
- Systems integration program assessments
- Enterprise data management strategy
- Merger integration planning /due diligence
- Network security, information assurance, & digital risk

Operation Model Strategy & Design
- Sarbanes Oxley applications
- Consolidation systems
- Procurement sourcing tools
- People Soft conversions
- Tax document management systems
- Document storage systems

PROFESSIONAL EXPERIENCE

BBC., New York, NY   **1998 to Present**
IT Director, New York and London (2003 to Present)
Provide applications systems support for six-department corporate division. Oversee management of close to 40 applications and lead team of developers in New York and London. Project Scope: $180K to $5M; Staff: 8

Led multimillion-dollar Sarbanes Oxley application keeping all phases of project on time and under budget.
- Trimmed $170K off phase one alone by effectively managing resources and eliminating need for additional consultants.
- Spearheaded due diligence process; audited ten different applications and developed prototype before launching project.
- Oversaw 16-person senior task force comprised of 8 corporate divisions to define requirements and develop proposal.
- Mitigated risk and corporate liability by developing robust security documentation process in compliance with SOX.
- Acted as "go to person" and sounding board for Information Security Senior Manager regarding all SOX issues.

Shaved millions of dollars off systems costs and eliminated need to replace corporate accounting shared server system by recommending and implementing migration to more robust People Soft product.
- Decommissioned redundant servers and reduced number of personnel needed to maintain systems.
- Created opportunity to outsource process and improve efficiencies.

Trimmed time spent locating and managing corporate tax department documentation by hundreds of hours annually by launching company's inaugural Treasury Workstation documentation management system.
- Improved firm's ability to source crucial tax breaks by installing a state and local planning system to identify regional tax structures and associated perks.
- Bolstered integrity and tracking of audit data by developing corporate division's first-ever internal audit tracking tool.
- Eliminated potential risk factors associated with mandatory auditing processes by developing guidelines for and reviewing meticulous documentation system designed to protect firm from potential misappropriation of funds.

EXAMPLE OF A TECHNOLOGY RÉSUMÉ

Saved millions of dollars for firm by implementing enterprise-wide procurement application to consolidate purchases and improve tracking mechanisms.
- Installed cost-saving features including an e-auction tool, shared contracts, and supplier analysis reporting features.

Elevated expectations for team accountability and project management resulting in virtually no occurrences of projects going over time or budget constraints.
- Streamlined communications between New York and London by developing monthly project reporting tool and promoting the corporate resources group in London to their New York counterparts.
- Saved significant time and eliminated document retrieval issues by creating a shared U.S./UK document storage system.
- Maximized communications across groups despite six-hour time difference; instilled project autonomy while giving developers increased lead time on projects and implementing systematic documentation guidelines.

IT Manager, New York, NY (2000 to 2003)
Managed all financial applications for multiple corporate departments including financial reporting and accounting policy, financial consolidation, budgeting and forecasting, purchasing, tax, treasury, real estate, corporate accounting, internal audit, and print shop. Support included process management, addressing security issues, application support, stress testing and systems auditing. Additionally tasked with managing vendor relationships and liaising with internal IT groups for implementation, upgrades, and maintenance. Project Scope: 100K; Staff: 5

- Partnered with IT team of recently acquired company to streamline and consolidate financial reporting tools in preparation for BTC/BBC merger; advised BBC on their rollout of consolidation tool, including centralized access for remote offices.
- Appointed acting VP for six-month period with responsibilities for a 13-person team, department budget, and internal/ external customer relationship management.
- Slashed close time for corporate UK Treasury and Tax by five days by consolidating financial reporting systems.
- Improved functionality of financial reporting systems for eight unique divisions; automated procedures, created seamless interface, customized solutions, centralizing systems, and developed training manuals and platform training program for 120 users; new standardized processes became the template for future consolidation efforts.
- Significantly improved document storage and tracking capabilities related to Sarbanes Oxley documentation by co-developing enterprise-wide e-Room document storage and management tools, which converted e-mail correspondence to a more sophisticated shared tracking database for 260 users.

Senior Applications Consultant, New York, NY (1998 to 2000)
Recruited from Intershare Inc. to become BBC's sole applications consultant for the financial consolidation systems.
- Tested and rolled-out Y2K version of consolidation tool (first mission critical application to pass Y2K testing).
- Developed new Excel-based front-end for consolidation tool.
- Provided all documentation for consolidation systems including user manual, IT manual, relevant install and support documentation, and systems development life-cycle documentation for upgrades.
- Trained users on implementation and usage of applications across divisions, created area on corporate Internet for consolidation application, and rolled out enterprise-wide portal allowing select access to CITRIX consolidation tool.

INTERSHARE INC., London, UK   1990 to 1998
Senior Applications Consultant, New York, NY (1997 to 1998)
Selected for U.S. consulting position working on consolidation systems for Fortune 500 companies. Provided general application support for AIG, Dover Corporation, Texaco, Time Inc., Time Warner Inc., and Toshiba American Consumer Products.
Project Leader, Management Support Systems, Paris, France (1993 to 1997)
Recruited for assignment with Corenet Inc. to provide front-line support for the corporate consolidation system.
- Created training database, documentation, user manual, and training program delivered to 150 users worldwide.
- Implemented General Ledger interface; U.S. with J.D. Edwards, Switzerland with SAP and Abacus.

EXAMPLE OF A TECHNOLOGY RÉSUMÉ

International Product Support Consultant, London, UK (1990 to 1993)
International support for retail and financial consolidation software products.

EDUCATION AND ONGOING PROFESSIONAL DEVELOPMENT

Certified Information Security Manager (CISM), New York, NY, 2006
BBC Leadership Development Program, London, UK, 2003
Management Skills for IT Professionals, New Horizons Computer Learning Center, New York, NY, 2000
B.A., Social Science, Middlesex Polytechnic, Middlesex, UK, 1990

TECHNOLOGY

Client, server, and mainframe operating systems, Microsoft Professional Office Suite, Microsoft FrontPage, Excel VBA, HTML, Adobe Acrobat, Visio, Hyperion Financial Products, J.D. Edwards FASTR, Citrix Metaframe and NFuse, peregrine and remedy call logging and change management programs, RIM Blackberry implementation.

CASE STUDY: BARBARA SAFANI

Barbara Safani spent eight years as an HR Manager for a Fortune 100 company, managing recruiting, organizational development, and employee relations initiatives. Next, she worked for an outplacement firm supporting organizations that were downsizing. She coached displaced employees on résumé writing, interviewing, and negotiation strategy. This led her to open her own career management firm specializing in these same services for retail rather than corporate clients. Her areas of expertise are résumé writing, job search coaching, and online identity campaigns.

Over the last decade, she has seen the Internet help job seekers create additional visibility for their candidacy and allow them to market themselves in more creative and strategic ways. She believes the Internet will continue to be used as a tool for sourcing candidates and validating their competencies. A strong Web presence will become a necessity for all job seekers and candidates, who will continue to find ways to become known through online communities, such as blogs and social networking sites.

Barbara feels that the most important thing is to have your résumé focus on quantifiable accomplishments rather than job tasks. Over the years, she has seen many mistakes made on résumés, and the worst things that people do are:

- Provide inaccurate or inflated information

- Focus on job tasks rather than accomplishments

- Use clichéd phrases such as "team player" or "good communicator" without substantiating these claims

CASE STUDY: BARBARA SAFANI

- Use clichéd phrases such as "team player" or "good communicator" without substantiating these claims

- Have misspelled words or grammatical errors

- Include a salary history or salary requirements

She offers the following suggestions to make the most of your résumé to get the job that is perfect for you:

- Include a career summary that quickly communicates your personal brand and the value you bring to the job

- Provide a list of core competencies or areas of strength

- Discuss accomplishments and qualify achievements using numbers, dollars, and percentages

- Proofread thoroughly

- Create a cover letter to build rapport with the reader and ask for the interview

She recommends keeping the document to one or two full pages. Use color gently and choose traditional colors for your paper. Make sure you do not use a font smaller than 10 point and use bolding and italics only to highlight key points. However, if you are sending your résumé electronically, you have to eliminate design elements, convert to plain text, and just use spacing and dashed lines to separate and highlight important text.

Savvy job seekers know how to leverage the Internet as part of their search campaign. They build visibility and community by blogging, commenting on other people's blogs, and participating in social networking communities, such as LinkedIn, Ecademy, Ryze, Facebook, and MySpace.

For today's job seekers, Safani offers this advice, "Stay abreast of current tools for networking. Build relationships with people who understand Web 2.0 technology and can teach you how to use these tools to improve the quality of your search."

Barbara Safani can be reached through her Web site — **www.careersolvers.com.**

CHAPTER 11:

ESPECIALLY FOR STUDENTS

Being a recent graduate is a special challenge in today's economy. The purpose of a résumé is to generate interest and to be invited to an interview. This document is not the story of your life.

- The challenge is to show value when you do not have an extensive work history to back it up.

- You need to understand the company's needs. If you know what the company is looking for, you can show them how you can give it to them.

- Create a value statement. This shows what you can offer potential employers.

- Create strong content that comes from your unique experiences and skills.

- Remember — work is work, whether it is paid or not. Include any volunteer work or helping a friend. Even skills that have been self-taught are valuable and need to go on a résumé.

The following is a series of worksheets to help you find out what you would like to do, the skills you would like to use, and the type of work you would enjoy doing.

LIFE STYLE WORKSHEET

List a couple of jobs that you would love to do: _____

LIFE STYLE WORKSHEET

Write down the type of work that you might find interesting. _____
_____

Write down the type of life style that you would like to live. _____
_____

Think about the skills you would like to use. _____
_____

What working environment would you like be a part of?_____
_____

What people would you like to work with? _____
_____

What work values do you have to meet? _____
_____

Where would you like to live? _____

What salary do you need to earn? _____

Where do you want to be in five years? _____
_____

Where do you want to be in ten years? _____
_____

FINDING YOUR SKILLS FROM LIFE EXPERIENCE

With each of the subjects listed below, search and identify several skills that you have learned from each one. Try to find between one and three skills for each. If an area does not apply to you, skip to the next one. This will help you find transferable and personal skills. We learn in many different ways. In each of the circumstances below, we have learned something. Those skills automatically transfer to other areas of your life.

School (high school/postsecondary):

1. _____
2. _____
3. _____

Work/Jobs (part-time/full-time/volunteer):

1. _____
2. _____
3. _____

FINDING YOUR SKILLS FROM LIFE EXPERIENCE

Community (associations/teams/neighborhood):

1. _____
2. _____
3. _____

Friends (good/bad/present/past):

1. _____
2. _____
3. _____

Family (include extended):

1. _____
2. _____
3. _____

Internet (learning/surfacing/interacting):

1. _____
2. _____
3. _____

Trial and Error (of everything):

1. _____
2. _____
3. _____

Sports/Education (teams/training/participating/observing):

1. _____
2. _____
3. _____

Religion (belonging/teaching/volunteering):

1. _____
2. _____
3. _____

Teachers (the good, the bad):

1. _____
2. _____
3. _____

FINDING YOUR SKILLS FROM LIFE EXPERIENCE

Day-to-day life (we learn something new every day):

1. _____
2. _____
3. _____

Peers/Colleagues (past/present):

1. _____
2. _____
3. _____

Observation (of others/yourself):

1. _____
2. _____
3. _____

A loved one (living/passed):

1. _____
2. _____
3. _____

Your life style and history:

1. _____
2. _____
3. _____

STRENGTHS WORKSHEET

Academic

Grades: _____   Special Products: _____

Test Results: _____   Honors: _____

Extra Information

Placements: _____   Additional Courses: _____

Related Work: _____   Internships: _____

Extracurricular

Sports: _____   Awards: _____

Recognition: _____   Teams: _____

STRENGTHS WORKSHEET

School Activities

School Leadership: _____   Position: _____

Publications: _____   Clubs: _____

Music: _____   Drama: _____

Other: _____   Other: _____

Other Activities

Community Service: _____   Work: _____

Work: _____   Work: _____

Volunteer: _____   Religious: _____

Political: _____   Travel: _____

Character Strengths

Empathy_____   Adaptability _____

Integrity _____   Optimism_____

Persistence_____   Creativity _____

Independence _____   Courage _____

Reliability _____   Concern for Others _____

Leadership _____   Modesty_____

Patience _____   Tolerance_____

Other_____   Other _____

Skills/Talents

1. _____
2. _____
3. _____

Like the other worksheets, use the following to find the accomplishments and activities to support your application. This can be for entrance to college, a job application, or any other type of competition, including a scholarship. This is also a good document to keep. Offer this worksheet or your finished résumé to anyone you are planning to ask to write you a letter of recommendation.

STUDENT RÉSUMÉ WORKSHEET

Name (as you want it to be on your résumé)

Address

City   **State**   **ZIP**

Phone number (number where an employer could call and leave a message); include area code

E-mail address

Web site (only if appropriate)

Graduation Year

Academic Information

Test Scores _____

GPA _____ Rank in Class _____

Honors/AP Courses _____

Education

Degree or Certificate

Majors/Minors or Course Highlights

School Name, City/State   **Year graduated or years enrolled**

Work Experience

Company Name, City, State   **Start and end date**

Job Title   **(Month/Year)**

STUDENT RÉSUMÉ WORKSHEET

Accomplishments:_____

_____

Work Experience

_____

Company Name, City, State   **Start and end date**

_____

Job Title   **(Month/Year)**

#2 Work Experience

_____

Company Name, City, State   **Start and end date**

_____

Job Title   **(Month/Year)**

Accomplishments:_____

_____

Activities and Sports
List here the activities and sports you are involved with, up to five major (relevant)
activities. Include position information and a brief description, length of time, and
time commitment in hours per week or month. _____

_____

_____

Leadership Positions
You can include those at school and other positions, if not already mentioned above.
Include when you held this position and what activities you were responsible for.____

_____

_____

Community Service
Include all volunteer work or any community efforts you took part in. Again, remember
to list what you did, when you did it, how long you were involved, and for whom.____

_____

_____

Honors and Awards
List the name of the award, year received, and include a brief description of the
reason for the award. _____

_____

_____

STUDENT RÉSUMÉ WORKSHEET

Special Hobbies or Interests

List any hobbies or interests that you are involved in — giving particular importance to those that are applicable.

_____

_____

_____

Education Goals

List graduate and undergraduate studies, diplomas, and licenses.

_____

_____

_____

Career Path

Explain where you are heading with your education pathway.

_____

_____

_____

Special Conditions

List any special conditions that you are dealing with, if any.

_____

_____

_____

SAMPLE STUDENT RÉSUMÉ

NAME
Address
City, State ZIP

Telephone Number
E-mail address
Graduation Year

SUMMARY

OBJECTIVE

EDUCATION

Dates attended
(Month/Year)

INSTITUTION NAME, City, State
Degree or Diploma
Specialization, Majors, Minors, or Area of
Concentration

Dates attended
(Month/Year)

INSTITUTION NAME, City, State
Degree or Diploma
Specialization, Majors, Minors, or Area of
Concentration

ACADEMIC ACHIEVEMENTS

(Month/Year)

Name of awards, issuing institution name
Name of awards, issuing institution name

SKILLS AND KNOWLEDGE ACQUIRED THROUGH EDUCATION AND EXPERIENCE

*
*
*

WORK EXPERIENCE

Company Name, City, State
Job Title

Start and end date

(Month/Year)

Accomplishments:

SAMPLE STUDENT RÉSUMÉ

Company Name, City, State   Start and end date
Job Title
                                                            (Month/Year)

Accomplishments:

VOLUNTEER EXPERIENCE

COMPANY NAME, City, State   Start and end date
Job Title
                                                            (Month/Year)

Accomplishments:

FUNCTIONAL SKILLS

•

•

PERSONAL SKILLS

•

•

EXTRACURRICULAR ACTIVITIES

•

•

INTERESTS

•

•

ADDITIONAL INFORMATION

•

•

References will be provided at the interview

CHAPTER 12:

THE FINAL CHECK

With all the time and effort you have put into creating your dynamic résumé, check to make sure it is as perfect as it can be. Remember, you have less than 30 seconds to make a favorable impression on a recruiter or hiring manager. Recruiters are looking for a reason to toss each résumé out. Do not give them that reason. Write your résumé well, check it over, edit it, check it over again, and have someone else look it over, too.

In her "Résumé Critique Checklist" article, Kim Isaacs offers some questions to ask yourself as you put the final finishes on your résumé:

CHECK IT FOR FIRST IMPRESSIONS

1. Does it look original, or does it look like every other résumé on the market?

2. Are there clear, easy-to-read sections? Can you see the sections at first glance?

3. Does it look professional?

4. Is there a summary or profile showing the reader what you have to offer?

5. Is it an appropriate length?

6. Is the contact information easy to see?

APPEARANCE

1. Does the résumé look good?

2. Does the résumé use a reasonable font size?

3. Have design elements been used appropriately? Do they help make the résumé easier to read?

4. Is there good use of white space?

5. Are the margins even and no smaller than 1″ and no larger than 1.5″?

6. Are the sections well spaced?

7. Are the fonts consistent and appropriately sized?

8. Have the headings and page breaks been used correctly?

9. Has appropriate quality 8 ½″ x 11″ paper been used?

10. If you have used color, has it been used sparingly?

EACH SECTION

1. Is each section heading clearly labeled and easy to read?

2. Are the sections relevant?

3. Check the order of the headings against the style of résumé you are using — is it correct?

CAREER GOAL

1. Is there a career objective at the top of the résumé in the qualifications summary?

2. Is this a targeted résumé? If so, have you taken care to focus your résumé to the particular job in question?

3. If this résumé is for a career change, is the current objective clearly listed with relevant details to support it?

ACCOMPLISHMENTS

1. Is the list of accomplishments powerful, yet easy to read?

2. Are there numbers, either percentages or dollar amounts, to support your accomplishments?

3. Have strong action verbs been used to start each sentence?

4. Did you use accomplishments instead of responsibilities?

5. Were descriptive (not necessarily actual) job titles listed?

EDUCATION

1. Did you list a major GPA, if over 3.0, and an overall GPA, if under 3.0?

2. Is there a projected graduation date listed if you are still in school?

3. Has your degree been listed first, then college or university name second?

RELEVANCE

1. Is everything on the résumé necessary?

2. Are the stated claims supported throughout?

3. Is the information relevant to the job description?

4. Does the information support the career objective?

5. Is the résumé packed with keywords and industry jargon?

6. Has personal information, like marital status and age, been left off?

FOCUS

1. Is the résumé consistent?

2. Does it respond to the employer's needs and requirements?

3. Is the résumé employer-focused and not "you"-focused?

4. Does it show insider knowledge of the problems and solutions of the industry?

WRITING STYLE

1. Is the writing easy to read and understand?

2. Does the content flow logically?

3. Have you left off personal pronouns, like I, me, and my?

4. Are there short, three- to five-sentence paragraphs?

5. Does it use brief and succinct language only?

6. Are there any typos or errors in language, spelling, or grammar?

7. Have you proven that you are the best candidate for this position?

TIPS AND TRICKS

When writing a document that can make or break your future, use any tips or tricks you can. Some of these points have been touched on before in the book, but they are also mentioned here to point out their relevance:

- Remember to use a proper e-mail address and not a "fun" one. Go plain and professional all the way.

- Avoid generic phrases, such as, "looking for a position in a large company where there is room to grow." Be specific.

- Spell check, but do not rely on a computer spell checker. Computers are great tools, but the spell checker will not pick up mistakes such as when to use "form" or "from."

- Tweak your résumé to show your relevant responsibilities and accomplishments.

- Do not be afraid to show your skills. This is not the time to be shy.

- Use multiple versions of your résumé to apply for different positions.

- Do not get too fancy — it is liable to backfire on you.

- Keep the résumé as short as possible.

- Have someone else check over your résumé. Give them 30 seconds and see if they feel you are truly qualified for the position.

CASE STUDY: JEREMY WORTHINGTON

Jeremy Worthington, CARW, is Creative Director of Buckeye Résumés, where he has received many tributes for the designs and presentation strategies that have distinguished his candidates in the career world. Jeremy was born into the job hunting industry. Growing up as the son of Janice Worthington, he was exposed to career information from the start. Throughout those years, he developed a passion for the industry and the family business.

As Worthington Career Services expanded, Jeremy, with his ten years of experience, opened Buckeye Résumés to specialize in a different clientele.

Over the years, he sees that résumés have become more comprehensive and direct; much more relevant to the positions they are meant for. Although technology has its place in the future of the job hunting industry, he firmly believes in face-to-face meetings as much as possible. It is not all about the Internet. Do create an ASCII version of your résumé if applying electronically, but structure it to look as much like a traditional résumé as possible. He can see change coming in the industry as it evolves and adapts to the changing needs of society.

CASE STUDY: JEREMY WORTHINGTON

Regardless of the changes in the industry, the fundamental issue is to connect your abilities to provide solutions to the needs of the employer. You do not want your résumé to be too flamboyant, full of errors, off the topic, irrelevant, arrogant, or full of personal information. Instead, keep it simple, get to the point, research what the company needs, and deliver your value to provide a solution to their problem. The biggest mistake people make is not knowing the difference between a generic or a targeted solution.

Retail manager = generic distribution

Men's shoe department manager = targeted

Here are his words of advice for the job hunter of today: "People have the 'deer staring in the headlights block.' Do not be one of them. Get a strategy, research as much as you can, then you will see the steps and dynamic approach to get where you want to go. The more informed you are, the better off we all are."

Jeremy Worthington can be contacted through his Web site, **www.buckeyeresumes. com.**

CHAPTER 13:

LETTERS, LETTERS, AND MORE LETTERS

Before writing and sending any letter, it helps to know what to do and what not to do, to whom you are writing the letter, the best type of letter, and a way to track when and to whom you have sent the letters. This ensures that you do not double up on your letters and it allows you to see when it is time for a follow up. You also need to know what you have said to each potential employer so it is helpful to keep a copy of each letter.

COVER LETTERS

OVERVIEW

A cover letter is the letter that accompanies your résumé. It introduces you to a potential employer.

While a cover letter is required, that does not guarantee that it will be read. Some recruiters and managers will pore over each line, and some will not even look at it. What this means is you have to write the best cover letter you can because you have to assume that someone will look at it.

Think, for a moment, about the employer who has to read through 400+ résumés and cover letters for every one of the jobs they post on a major job site, like **Monster.com**. What does it take to have your résumé make the cut and not land in the trash can?

Every employer has to find a way to reduce these applications down to a reasonable, manageable level. Understanding how they do it helps you understand what you can do to avoid being weeded out.

If your cover letter and résumé are not perfect, they will be rejected. That means no typos, spelling, or grammatical errors. If your qualifications are not obvious at first glance, you will be rejected. So make the information that they need to see easily accessible.

It is up to you to make a good impression. Their first glance is the one chance you have to make it to the next round.

One of the best ways to do this is to list the criteria on the job posting and then list the skills and experience that you have that match the job criteria. You need to either address how your skills match the job in a written paragraph or list them.

This can be done with only one type of cover letter. Even though there are a variety of styles and content elements that make up a cover letter, there are only two basic formats.

PURPOSE

A cover letter should be a brief introduction — not a complete history. Keep it short and simple. However, make sure it lets the employer know:

1. What position you are applying for

2. Your key selling points

3. That you understand the needs of the employer

4. Your contact information

THE DOS AND DON'TS

There are important basics to understand about writing letters of all kinds. With the importance of your career's future at stake, this is no time to ignore business standards.

Do:

- Follow the layout and format of a standard business letter.

- Focus the letter on what you can offer the prospective employer.

- Personalize whenever possible. Check the spelling and title of the individual.

- Spell check, proofread, and use standard punctuation and paragraphs for both e-mail and print cover letters.

- Make sure you do not copy someone else's cover letter. Write one for yourself in your own words.

- Use informal, conversational-style language.

- Sign the cover letter.

- Use good quality paper.

- Be concise and to the point in your wording.

- Close with a call to action, like a request for a meeting.

- If you know someone in the company, you can mention this person's name.

Do not:

- Use stiff or awkward language.

- Try anything unorthodox.

- Be arrogant or superior about your skills.

- Overuse the word "I."

- Say how lucky the company would be if you worked for them.

- Inflate your capabilities and qualities.

- Use Internet chat language in the letter or e-mail.

- Use acronyms that might not be understood.

Do not waste your time and everyone else's — if you do not have the qualifications, do not apply. Instead, focus on jobs that you are qualified for and even consider taking courses or additional training so you will have the qualifications for the next opportunity.

BROADCAST LETTER

This type of letter is used to announce your availability to many employers at the same time without having to compose a separate letter for each one. This is not the same letter used to apply for a specific job. That does not mean you start it with a generic address and content that would apply to any industry. Make sure it is personalized. Add in a phrase that tailors the writing to the type of industry and position you are hoping to find. If you are considering this type of letter, it usually means that you do not have any specific job details and must make it more general. Here is one example:

I am writing to highlight my credentials for a position in…

This is a simple way to tailor a letter without writing individually targeted letters.

THE TARGETED COVER LETTER

This type of cover letter is used to apply for a specific job. This could be answering a job ad or introducing yourself after hearing about an open position through a friend. This type of letter is used when you know the details about the position. With this information, you can show how your abilities can match the needs of the company. It also gives you an opportunity to reference specific information about the company. Take the time to research the company and learn a little about what they do, how they do it, and what their values are. This will not only give you much needed information, but it will also allow you the opportunity to see if this is a company where you would like to work. It is a good idea to include a comment on the cover letter that shows you have done some research on the company.

I was impressed with the success of your new product launch...

Remember that, just like a résumé, a cover letter needs to show your value to the recruiter or hiring manager.

INQUIRY LETTER

An inquiry letter is for when you do not have a specific job in mind and have done research on various companies that you would like to work for. You then write the letter requesting employment information. Make sure your research has been extensive enough to write with some degree of knowledge.

In this type of letter:

- Take the time to write to a specific person in the company. In larger organizations, you can send it to:

    a)   Personnel Department

    b)   Human Resources Department

    c)   Manager of Employment

    d)   Recruitment

If you can address the inquiry letter to a specific department manager, all the better. If you have to make it a general address, you can use:

    a)   Dear Madam or Sir

    b)   Dear Selection Committee Chair

- Make sure to state your interest in the organization. Be specific about the type of position you are looking for.

- Finish with information as to when you are available for an interview and where you can be reached.

SAMPLE COVER LETTER - STANDARD

Your Name
Your Current Address
City, State, ZIP Code
E-mail Address

Date

Ms. Gotajob
Title
Organization
Street Address
City, State, ZIP Code

Dear Ms. Gotajob:

First Paragraph — Explain why you are writing the letter. Include the name of the position or the general career area about which you are inquiring. Tell how you heard about the opening.

Second Paragraph — Mention two to three of the most relevant skills or qualifications that would be of interest to the organization. Explain why you are interested in their company and this type of work. If this job means relocating, explain why the location is of interest. Make sure you mention if you have completed any specialized training or have directly related experience. Reference the ad and refer to your résumé included in the application package.

Third Paragraph — Finish with a request for a chance to visit the employer and speak further. Let them know that you will follow up with a phone call. Make sure your closing is a "call to action" for the reader. Thank the reader for considering your application.

Sincerely,

Your signature

Type your name
Enclosures

SAMPLE PROFESSIONAL COVER LETTER

BRADLEY BUCKINGHAM

1763 Raleigh Place • Merrick, NY 11566 • O: 516-570-4022 • C: 516-755-8811
bradley@buck.com

April 20, 2007
James LaRoche, VP, Web Development, Raines Media
60 West 44th Street
New York, NY 10036

Dear Mr. LaRoche:

"The Internet is becoming the town square for the global village of tomorrow" (Bill Gates). It is truly amazing how the Internet has brought people and ideas together in an effort to connect, exchange ideas, and offer products and services. With the advent of the technology, everyone has rushed to get on the Web marketing "bandwagon" to promote their wares. But with so much noise in cyberspace, **it can be hard to know how to position a product or service so a prospective buyer can find you and be receptive to your marketing message.**

That is where I come in. As a **web developer and online branding specialist**, I develop unique Web sites that cut through the clutter and get noticed by a target or niche audience. At the core of my consultative approach is my interest in understanding how your customer thinks. Through the process of discovery and persona/scenario development, I gather the necessary information to build Web sites that garner attention from those most interested in my clients' services. **My consultative approach helps me create sites that not only sell products, but provide touch points and communities for visitors that encourage them to return to the site**. After customer loyalty is attained, I focus on ways to continue to make the community an efficient and pleasant environment where information is accessible and purchasing options are easy to find and navigate.

I built such a community for **Sweet Scents**, a product with no previous Web presence. Instead of developing a site to simply market the product, I launched a unique community with ongoing synergies to attract interest and build brand loyalty. Through a sponsorship with ML International modeling agency, I marketed a model search contest, newsletter, and blog to **accelerate visitors to 200,000 within the first year.**

For **Hale and Hearty** fast food restaurant chain, I reviewed user behavior patterns, Web site usability, server analytics, and click path tracking to create a marketing strategy to capture new market share and **more than triple the number of visitors to the site in one year.** My clients also come to me when their current Web strategy just is not working. Prior to hiring me, **JRJ Investigators**, a private investigation firm, had spent two years trying to generate sales leads via their Web site with absolutely

SAMPLE PROFESSIONAL COVER LETTER

no success. By reworking the site's copy and analyzing the behaviors and buying patterns most associated with the agency's target audience, **I helped this client move from zero leads to 10 to 25 each month.**

After following your company for quite some time, I believe that your organization's message and brand are in synch with my career aspirations. I would welcome the chance to meet with you to discuss my qualifications in more detail and look forward to a personal interview.

Sincerely,

Bradley Buckingham
Bradley Buckingham

Attachment

*This cover letter was supplied by Barbara Safani of **CareerSolvers.com***

SAMPLE E-MAIL COVER LETTER

To: Recruiter or Hiring Manager's Name and E-mail

From: Your Name and E-mail Address

Subject: Office Manager's Position for Marker, Inc.

Dear Ms. Gotajob,

First Paragraph — Explain why you are writing the letter. Include the name of the position or the general career area about which you are inquiring. Tell how you heard about the opening.

Second Paragraph — Mention two to three of the most relevant skills or qualifications that would be of interest to the organization. Explain why you are interested in their company and the type of work. If this job means relocating, explain why the location is of interest. Make sure you mention if you have completed any specialized training or have directly related experience. Reference the ad and refer to your résumé included in the application package.

Third Paragraph — Finish with a request for a chance to visit the employer and speak further. Let them know that you will follow up with a phone call. Make sure your closing is a "call to action" for the reader. Thank the reader for considering your application.

Sincerely,

Type your name

WHEN RESPONDING TO AN AD OR JOB POSTING

When applying to a particular job ad, it is important to read the ad carefully. You need to understand what the company is looking for, what its needs are, and the skills required for the job. When you know these things, tailor the cover letter to answer them. Make sure you:

- Follow the ad's instructions carefully. Some companies want you to e-mail your résumé, others want you to go to their Web site, and others want the résumé mailed. They may request salary expectations, potential start date, and references.

- Make the letter brief but to the point.

- Make the letter personalized and factual.

- Put down your most relevant accomplishments and skills.

- Try to make your letter sound individualized and original.

- Act professional at all times. Stick to the facts, and make sure you can back up what you say.

SAMPLE AD AND COVER LETTER

OFFICE MANAGER. Keep detailed monthly expenses. Update weekly reports and distribute to department heads. Take notes during meetings, create and distribute monthly newsletter. Handle staff hiring and training. Monitor day-to-day work activities and schedule switchboard coverage. This position will be responsible for all ordering of office materials, staff holidays, organizing major company events, and both accounts receivable and accounts payable. Needs to have intermediate skills with Microsoft Office.

Here is the main paragraph of a cover letter written in two separate styles to respond to the above ad.

Cover Letter Example 1: Paragraph Style

As Office Manager for a local construction company, I was responsible for all office functions, including all the booking, updating, generating reports, and hiring and training our office staff of three. In addition, I was responsible for the day-to-day running of the business and organizing the monthly staff meetings and the annual Christmas party. I am proficient in Microsoft Office.

Cover Letter Example 2: List Style

This is the same response, only now written in a list format.

Office Manager Requirements:

- Take notes and generate meeting reports.

- Perform accounting activities, including accounts payable and accounts receivables.

- Generate and maintain reports.

- Hire, train, and supervise staff.

SAMPLE COVER LETTER WHEN RESPONDING TO AN AD

Your Name
Your Current Address
City, State, ZIP Code
E-mail Address

Date:

Re: Application for Office Manager

Ms. Gotajob
Title
Marker, Inc.
Street Address,
City, State, ZIP Code

Dear Ms. Gotajob,

I am interested in applying for the position of Office Manager for your company, Marker, Inc., which was advertised in the *Seattle Times* newspaper last Thursday, July 26th.

SAMPLE COVER LETTER WHEN RESPONDING TO AN AD

As Office Manager for a local construction company, I was responsible for all office functions, including all the booking, updating, generating reports, and hiring and training our office staff of three. In addition, I was responsible for the day-to-day running of the business and organizing the monthly staff meetings and the annual Christmas party. I am proficient in Microsoft Office.

I would enjoy a chance to join your team. Thank you for considering my application. I am available for an interview at your convenience. You can contact me at 555-1234. I look forward to hearing from you.

Sincerely,

Your signature
Type your name

Enclosures

INTERVIEW APPRECIATION LETTER

This is the traditional thank-you e-mail or letter sent after an interview. The purpose is to thank the interviewer for his or her time and remind him or her of who you are. When you write this letter, remember to:

- Thank the interviewer for his or her time and consideration.

- State the date of the interview.

- Mention your interest in working for the company.

- Address anything you may have forgotten during the interview.

- Ask any questions that you may not have asked or that may not have been answered during the interview.

- Express interest in when a decision might be reached.

SAMPLE INTERVIEW APPRECIATION LETTER

Your Name
Your Current Address
City, State, ZIP Code

E-mail Address

Date

Ms. Gotajob
Title
Organization
Street Address
City, State, ZIP Code

Dear Ms. Gotajob,

Thank you for taking the time to discuss the position of Office Manager in your Seattle office with me last Monday, July 18th. After meeting with you and having a chance to observe the office in question, I am convinced that my background and skills are a good fit for your needs.

In addition to my directly related experience and qualifications, I bring excellent work habits and people skills to the job. Your office is a full-service business, and will be a good learning environment and also a fun way to learn more about the industry. Thank you for the time you took in explaining how your company operations work.

I look forward, Ms. Gotajob, to hearing from you concerning your decision on this position. Again, I thank you for your time and consideration.

Sincerely,

Your signature
Your name

LETTER OF ACKNOWLEDGEMENT

When you receive an offer from a company, it is important to respond as soon as possible. It is not necessary to answer the offer with a "yes" or "no" at this time, but do acknowledge receipt and appreciation for the offer. In this letter:

- Acknowledge receipt of the offer

- Show appreciation for the offer

- Give the potential employer a date by which you will have made your decision

---

SAMPLE LETTER OF ACKNOWLEDGEMENT

Your Name
Your Current Address
City, State, ZIP Code
E-mail Address

Date:

Re: Application for Office Manager

Ms. Gotajob
Title
Marker Inc.
Street Address,
City, State, ZIP Code

Dear Ms. Gotajob,

Thank you for offering me the position of Office Manager for your Seattle office at a salary of $40,000 per year. I am excited about the opportunity to join your company.

I understand that I must notify you of my decision by the end of the month. I will contact you before then.

I appreciate your confidence. Thank you for the job offer.

Sincerely,

Your signature
Your name

LETTER OF ACCEPTANCE

If you decide to accept the offer, notify the company as soon as possible. You do not have to wait until the time you may have told them you would make a decision. The company will appreciate your promptness.

What you should do in an acceptance letter:

- Acknowledge the receipt of the offer, state whether the offer was made by letter, phone call, or meeting, and when it occurred.

- Be specific. Name the supervisor's name, salary mentioned, and list all other items mentioned and agreed to in the offer.

- Let them know your possible start date.

- Acknowledge if the offer is contingent on the completion of a course, degree, certification, or physical examination.

- State any questions you may have.

- Express appreciation for the offer.

- Ask whether any other information is required.

SAMPLE LETTER OF ACCEPTANCE

Your Name
Your Current Address
City, State, ZIP Code
E-mail Address

Date:

Re: Application for Office Manager

Ms. Gotajob
Title
Marker, Inc.
Street Address

City, State, ZIP Code

Dear Ms. Gotajob,

Thank you for the wonderful phone call this morning when you offered me the position of Office Manager at your Seattle location. Please consider this letter my formal acceptance.

I am pleased to accept your offer at an annual salary of $40,000.

As we agreed over the phone, my start date will be August 14th.

SAMPLE LETTER OF ACCEPTANCE

I understand that I will receive full pay during the three-month training period and that my company benefits will start on the day following the end of my probationary period.

Thank you again for this opportunity, and I look forward to joining your team. If there is any paperwork that I need to take care of, please let me know.

Sincerely,

Your signature
Your name

LETTER OF DECLINATION

It is a matter of courtesy to send out a letter of declination if you are rejecting a job offer. It may not be an easy letter to write, but the employer needs to know your decision. This type of letter is usually a formality, making your decision a matter of record for their files. It usually follows a phone call and avoids any confusion that may have arisen during the call.

With this letter:

- Show appreciation for the offer.

- State the exact position or title that you were offered.

- Answer as soon as possible.

SAMPLE DECLINATION LETTER

Your Name
Your Current Address
City, State, ZIP Code
E-mail Address

Date

Ms. Gotajob
Title

SAMPLE DECLINATION LETTER

Organization
Street Address
City, State, ZIP Code

Dear Ms. Gotajob,

Thank you for offering me the position of Office Manager for your Seattle location. I am certain that the position would be an exciting work opportunity.

I appreciate your offer; however, after careful thought, I must respectfully decline your job offer. I feel that a different job opportunity is a better match for my qualifications and career goals.

Again, I thank you for you offer. It was a pleasure to meet you and your staff.

Sincerely,

Your signature
Your name

THE OTHER LETTERS

There is much confusion about letters of recommendation, reference letters, commendation letters, evaluation letters, and the many other letters surrounding job hunting.

The terms reference letter or letter of recommendation are often used interchangeably. However, they are different. A letter of recommendation is written for a specific reader and is specific in nature. A reference letter is general in nature and is written for a general audience.

LETTERS OF RECOMMENDATION

There are two kinds of recommendation letters: Employment-related and postsecondary-school related.

Employment-Related

This is also called a recommendation letter (not a reference letter, as many people believe). The person the letter is being written about specifically requests this letter. These are normally positive letters and are written by someone who knows the person well enough to be able to comment on their skills, abilities, and specific work qualities.

This employment-related recommendation letter is one person's view of the second person's work performance and skill base. Usually, the person writing the letter has been supervising the other person in the general workplace.

These letters are often asked for by potential employers or bigger bosses who are considering this person for a promotion. They are often addressed to one specific person — the potential employer or interested boss.

POSTSECONDARY-SCHOOL RELATED

Recommendation letters are a common requirement for entry into university and college postgraduate programs. It is common for graduate programs to request two or more letters of recommendation as part of their admission requirements.

Again, these types of letters are requested of an individual who is familiar with the applicant's academic history, current career, and future educational aspirations. These letters are asked of faculty members, administrators, and academic supervisors.

These letters are also addressed to a specific person and are to be included in the program admission application, along with the résumé and other requested documentation.

CHARACTER REFERENCE LETTER

These letters are similar to the standard reference letter, but can be required by a new employer if the line of work involves performing personal and home-based services, such as nannies, daycare, and domestic services.

These types of letters are written by previous employers and talk about the person's character, honesty, dependability, and work ethic.

COMMENDATION LETTERS

These are letters that a person writes to commend a coworker or employee to their manager when that person has done something outstanding. These are commonly written by someone other than the immediate supervisor; they are usually from someone from another area or who is visiting and was impressed by this person.

Again, these types of letters lend weight to your résumé and people tend to send them as part of an application package in hopes that they will make a difference.

EVALUATION LETTERS

These are detailed assessments of a person's work performance, done as part of the company's review process. When complete, these types of letters are put into the person's personnel file. A copy is often given to the employee for his or her own safekeeping.

It is not usual to send these in as part of your job package; however, if the results and comments are outstanding, they do give weight to your words in a job interview.

GENERAL LETTER OF REFERENCE

These are the more common letters of reference and are for letters that do not fit into the above categories. The general letter is often requested by employees when they leave an organization. They normally start, "To whom it may concern," and give a basic overview of the employee's work history, employment dates, job title(s), credentials, and anything else pertinent to the employee's stay at the company. These letters generally are positive and give a statement about the employee's work record.

These letters are often submitted with job applications with the hope that they will support the résumé in a favorable light and increase the chances of getting the applied-for position.

CHAPTER 14:

PORTFOLIOS

A portfolio is a collection of works that provide evidence of a person's skills. It is a way for job seekers to show they are a viable candidate for a position. Traditionally, when we think of the portfolio, we think of a person struggling with an oversize case containing artwork. By today's standards, this portfolio can include a résumé, reports, lesson plans, transcripts, certifications, letters, or samples of any particular type of work. It can also be in paper or electronic form.

An online portfolio provides a way to display your work and accomplishments on a global level in an easily accessible form through the Internet. A graphic design portfolio is a necessity if you are a freelance graphic designer or doing desktop publishing work — unless of course, yours is a household name and you are swamped with work.

For those job seekers currently looking for work, you will need a portfolio and a résumé.

THE PURPOSE OF A PORTFOLIO

When you create a strong portfolio, you are giving evidence of the scope and quality of your training and the work experience you have gained so far. This collection is an organized documentation of your personal and professional achievements.

Portfolios come in varying degrees of difficulty; they range from something simple, like putting your résumé online, to creating a Web site full of your work. These portfolios can include your writing samples, digital images of your graphic designs and artwork, video and audio files, and even transcripts and awards.

CREATING A PORTFOLIO

Creating an online portfolio depends on your own computer skills. As your goal is to present your work in a professional yet pleasing manner to the viewer in looks and functionality, you may want to consider the services of portfolio specialists. They would discuss your needs and build a site designed for you where you can simply upload your documents.

There are currently several Web sites that allow portfolios to be stored online free along with your free Web hosting. These "free" options are limited in the size and amount that you can upload; therefore, most Web hosting sites have specially designed portfolio options for a small fee. One of these sites is **www.Portfolios.com**.

These services are only an option. If you can build your own Web site or have someone help you do the design work, designing your own portfolio might be the way to go.

Remember that some portfolios are just classy layouts converted to a PDF and uploaded to a Web site. Other portfolios are several Web pages long and others, for the programmers and techies, are Web sites, complete with functionality and fun user experiences incorporated.

HOW LONG IS A PORTFOLIO?

The length of your portfolio depends on your discipline, years of experience, and the level of the position to which you are applying.

It is better to make it slightly longer and include what you feel is necessary than to feel you should have added something based on a question you have just been asked by an interviewer.

Some suggest that ten pages is appropriate for a portfolio, not including an introduction or the table of contents. Up to 20 pages is normal if you have a diverse and extensive skill set to offer. For a paper portfolio, keeping the number of pages down will help keep the costs down. When you explore online portfolios or portfolios on CDs or DVDs, the size of a portfolio is a different matter.

HOW TO USE A PORTFOLIO

It is a good idea to let a prospective employer know that you are planning to bring your portfolio to the interview. This can be done in your cover letter or résumé:

> "References and portfolio will be available at the interview."

> "My professional portfolio is available on request."

Your portfolio is meant to answer questions, but invariably it will create many more. Look over the portfolio and try to anticipate any questions that you might be asked. Take the time to practice answering them before you get to the interview.

Learn the portfolio inside and out. Learn to be comfortable pointing out items, shuffling through the pieces, and remembering the highlights to tell the hiring manager. This will boost your self-confidence, which will show in your interview.

During the interview, show your portfolio within the first 15 minutes. Ask, "May I show you some samples of my work?" or something similar. Make sure you display your items in such a way that the interviewer can see them. Turn the pieces or walk around the desk to give them a better picture. Be careful not to dominate the interview. The portfolio is a tool to help you answer questions but not to take over. Watch the interviewer for clues as to how you are doing.

After the interview, take the time to assess how you did. Look at any improvements you can make for the next interview.

The more you use your portfolio, the more natural it becomes to have it.

TIPS FOR THE PORTFOLIO

Here are some additional tips to help make your portfolio as good as it can be:

- Make it interesting and easy to read.

- Use action verbs to start your sentences.

- Do not lie.

- Use bullets for easier reading.

- Be sure to use easy-to-read fonts.

- Do not overuse extras (bold, italics, underlining, or all capitals).

- Have someone else proofread the portfolio.

- Make good use of white space.

- Use wide margins.

- Be consistent.

- Add a bit of color to break up the whiteness.

- Only use good quality copies and materials.

Once again, the thing to remember is this is a marketing tool, and like your résumé, your portfolio needs to present you and your skills in a strong and professional way.

PORTFOLIO PRESENTATION

The presentation of your portfolio is important and as individualized as the industry to which you are applying.

HARD COPY VERSION

As a portfolio is intended to enhance your professional qualities, it must be presented in the same manner.

Here are some tips for presentation:

- Make it reader friendly.

- Keep it short and concise.

- Avoid repetition.

- Use good quality, standard size 8 ½" x 11" paper.

- Use a professional binder — consider leather or synthetic leather.

- Use an appropriate business color, such as gray, black, brown, or navy. Avoid letting your creative thinking take you out of the professional box at this point.

- Use plastic page covers.

- Organize the portfolio in a logical manner appropriate for your discipline.

- Include a table of contents and tabs for easy navigation, depending on the size of the portfolio.

PDF VERSION

This type of format can be the copies from your paper portfolio scanned in, formatted in a program like Word, Publisher, or PageMaker, depending on the resources you have available, and then converted to a PDF for either posting on a Web site or e-mailing on request.

ELECTRONIC VERSION

Alongside your traditional portfolio, it is a good idea to create an electronic portfolio. This type of portfolio can then be a supplement to your traditional résumé. The portfolio can be on the Internet, CD, DVD, floppy, or zip drive. Using this type of portfolio allows you to use PowerPoint to make presentations. This type of format removes the size restriction but increases the need for organization of your portfolio. Using an electronic portfolio demonstrates your computer savvy and familiarity with newer technology.

It is a good idea to finish your traditional portfolio first and then work on creating an electronic version. Use word processing files for the various writing samples, scan in all the photographs, artwork, awards, and transcripts, and include any brochures or event programs you may have.

Now with the traditional material online, you can expand the functionality and aesthetics through audio, video clips, e-mail links, and external links to relevant sites.

Remember to keep only professional material here and not personal information or photos. As such, you might want to consider hosting the portfolio on a separate server from where your Web site is located. Some people consider an online portfolio the same thing as a personal Web site dedicated to their profession or a Web résumé. Each of these styles has similarities, and it is what you put on the pages that defines the name and usage.

You can also post your portfolio with dedicated services that allow you to direct someone to view your work on their site.

TYPES OF PORTFOLIOS

Because there are many different styles of portfolios, it is easier to discuss them individually.

JOB SEARCH OR PROFESSIONAL EMPLOYMENT PORTFOLIO

The job search portfolio is a new twist on an old tradition. Originally the domain of graphic artists, journalists, and teachers, it has become a common tool for job seekers and might be called a job skills, job search, or professional portfolio. It allows you to provide a bigger picture of who you are than a cover letter or résumé can. This career portfolio can be used in an interview to demonstrate your skills, illustrate the depth of your knowledge, and point out your accomplishments.

Like any portfolio, this one should be maintained and updated on a regular basis. The hardest part is the initial creation, when you have to decide on the format and the organization of the content. As with other portfolios, keep the portfolio in a 3-inch binder and use some navigation system, like tabs or dividers. For this type of portfolio, it is also a good idea to create an online portfolio as well.

If done well, a professional portfolio will:

- Highlight your achievements

- Show the diversity and quality of your work

- Emphasize your skills and abilities

- Set you apart from other candidates

- Illustrate your style and creative potential

- Support what you say in your interview

WHAT GOES IN THIS TYPE OF PORTFOLIO?

Determining what goes into your portfolio will be decided in part by the type of interview and the questions you think you might be asked. When you have considered these questions, choose items from your portfolio to help you answer them. Some items to consider include:

- **Career Summary** — This statement says what you stand for in terms of work philosophy, organizational interests, and often will include a comment on where you see yourself in five years.

- **Mission Statement** — A concise statement about the principles that drive your career path.

- **Résumé** — Include your current résumé.

- **Scannable Résumé** — Include a text-only version.

- **Accomplishments** — A list of your major career highlights.

- **Work Samples** — Include your best work to date, including presentations, papers, brochures, projects, and material on CDs or other multimedia.

- **Publications** — Include any published papers.

- **Testimonials** — Include any favorable employer evaluations and reviews, customer comments, or recognition of any kind that you have received.

- **Letters of Recommendation** — Include any that you have.

- **Honors and Awards** — Include any certificates or awards and scholarships you may have received.

- **Conferences/Workshops** — List the ones that you gave, participated in, or attended.

- **Education** — Include transcripts, degrees, licenses, and certifications along with a brief description of each, if required.

- **Professional Associations** — List any associations that you are a member of and any professional development programs you have completed.

- **Military Records** — List your military service, if applicable, and be sure to include any awards or honors received.

- **Volunteer Work** — Include any volunteer activities or pro bono work as it relates to your career.

- **References** — List between three and five (make sure to include full names, titles, addresses, and phone/e-mail). Make sure you have spoken to these people and they have confirmed that they will speak to your strengths, skills, and abilities.

- Writing samples

- Letters of commendation

- Documentation of technical or computer skills

- Newspaper articles or press releases relating to you and/or your work

- Internship or co-op reports

- Artwork showing your creativity

- Photographs demonstrating special skills

These are only some of the items that may apply to your discipline. There are many other options. Think about what would impress a potential employer and then find a piece that matches and include it with the rest.

For each job interview, reconsider the same question as to what you should include. Be sure to focus your portfolio to match the individual job.

GRAPHIC DESIGN PORTFOLIO

A graphic portfolio needs to be more than just a few scattered samples tossed into a folder. You want to choose the work that shows your skills to their best advantage. Having said that, if there is a piece that you do not love, leave it out. Chances are, when questioned abut it, you will inadvertently display some of your negativity.

If possible, use actual samples. If you have done jobs for clients and requested copies of print runs for yourself, add one to your portfolio. If you do not usually request copies, consider this a way to build a portfolio. You might be able to get one or two copies free. However, it is common to pay for extra copies. You can stipulate in your contracts how many portfolio pieces you will receive.

Include tear sheets. These are the torn-out ads, illustrations, and articles from original publications, such as magazines and newspapers, that are your own work.

Use copies if you cannot get originals. Use the proofs printed from your files or make the best quality color copies of the originals.

Take photographs of work too large to fit into the binder. This includes wall paintings, billboard ads, and large boxes.

If your work is in Web design or other electronic media, you can use it for a printed portfolio. Take screen shots of the work and print the Web pages. The only concern with this is that the screen resolution might not print out crisp and clear.

FOR THE FIRST-TIME PORTFOLIO CREATOR

Like any industry in which you need to show experience to get the job but you need the job to get experience, portfolios are no different. You need a portfolio to get a job, and you need the job to have something to put into the portfolio.

Here are some tips to help you create a portfolio:

- **Make up samples in graphic design.** It might feel like cheating, but in actuality, it shows what you can do, even if you did not do it for someone else.

- **Put in your pieces from your own business.** Feel free to use your own graphics and forms.

- **Put in pieces, such as holiday or birthday cards, that you might have made for friends, family, or just for fun.** Do you have graphics on a fun, personal Web site?

- **Use designs that were rejected by a client.** If you needed to create several pieces for a client until they find the design they like, the other designs can be used in your portfolio.

- **Use training pieces.** It is easiest to learn to use new software by doing. Use the finished pieces for your own portfolio.

- **Use assignment pieces.** If you have taken courses, seminars, or workshops and needed to develop something for these, use the samples for your portfolio.

As you create new pieces, upgrade your portfolio to showcase your best work.

HOW TO PRESENT THIS TYPE OF PORTFOLIO

Now that you have all your best pieces selected, find a professional way to present them. Many people use only a binder and plastic covers. Make sure you choose a good quality binder and covers. The cheap ones look … well, cheap.

You are applying for a job, but you do not want to seem desperate.

Other people purchase a portfolio case. If you decide to do this, make sure you choose one large enough to store your portfolio pieces without folding them.

If you buy one that is too large, they are awkward to work with, to show clients, and to travel with. Consider where you will be taking this portfolio when you determine the appropriate size.

HOW TO ORGANIZE YOUR PORTFOLIO PIECES

Now that you have all your best pieces and a case to put them in, you need to organize the pieces. Here are several suggestions for possible organization methods. Choose the one that suits you and the situation the best.

- **Put the best one first** — This method has you organizing material from your most favorite to your least favorite. The disadvantage of this method is that what you like best will not match the preferences of the person who is looking at them. Also, consider that the pieces can seem disconnected from each other.

- **Organize by technique** — Depending on the type of position you are applying for, you can sort your portfolio pieces by techniques, putting the most relevant first.

- **Organize by style** — Organize by style of design. Put the best and most relevant pieces first, as you do not know when the interviewer will have seen enough.

- **Sort by type** — With this method, you can put the types of graphic designs together. You could put brochures together, followed by letterhead designs or logos and business cards.

Make sure the pieces can be handled by the other person and consider having a good color copy to leave behind for them to keep.

ART AND PHOTOGRAPHY PORTFOLIOS

An art portfolio, the more traditional use of a portfolio, is necessary if you are looking to increase your client base, apply for work in your field, or be represented in a gallery. This packaging and presentation plays just as large a part as the contents of the portfolio.

- Your photographs and artwork must be professional.

- Pick out only finished prints; never show work prints or unspotted prints.

- Show your best work.

- Put careful thought and planning into a portfolio.

- Have continuity between images.

- Have a vision and make the portfolio represent that vision.

- Organize contents by subject or style.

- Keep black-and-white photos away from color photos for easier viewing.

- Organize horizontal, vertical, and different-size prints separately.

- Keep your portfolio in an appropriate case.

- Your photographs should be sale ready.

- They should be overmatted, signed, dated, titled, numbered, and stamped with your identification stamp.

- Be sure the overmats are clean and fingerprint free.

- Window overmats should be well cut with clean, straight lines.

EDITING YOUR WORK

Consider having someone else look over your portfolio and point out changes that could be made. It is difficult to edit your own work and even harder to be objective about your own photographs. You want to be sure your work gives a strong impression.

Limit the number of pieces in your portfolio to between ten and twenty. The objective is to introduce your work and to show the scope of your capabilities and the diversity of your creativity. Show your strongest work first.

See Appendix A, "Rules of the Road," for further information specific to editing photo and art portfolios.

CASE STUDY: DENNIS DUNLEAVY

Dennis Dunleavy is a college professor with close to 20 years of experience as a photojournalist and correspondent. He started out as a darkroom technician for an accident photographer in New York. From this point, he went on to gain valuable experience working as a freelance photographer for several years before joining a small Michigan newspaper as chief photographer. He also worked as a correspondent and as a writer. He currently teaches classes on visual journalism and reporting.

Over the last decades, he has watched technology open the door for people who may not otherwise have had the opportunity to break into photojournalism. He says anyone with a digital camera and a Flickr account online can have his or her work published commercially. Some of the most interesting changes he has seen in today's job-hunting world are in the presentation of multimedia packages.

"This means that still, audio, and video are presented to clients and potential employers to demonstrate versatility and depth for online markets. Almost all portfolios will be presented on CD or DVD instead of the traditional 'book' format. At the same time, there will continue to be room for niche specialists across an array of media platforms."

With the many changes happening in the industry, Dunleavy suggests learning to be good at business. Be organized and proactive. Do not wait for the phone to ring; keep pushing and trying to improve yourself. Build a network around you to gain experience, which in turn will lead to better, more highly paid jobs.

When asked for the worst portfolio mistakes, he offered these items:

1. Poorly edited writing and pictures.

2. Putting too many images and too many poor images into a portfolio. Include only your best work based on the needs and interests of a potential employer.

3. Not seeking second and third opinions before sending the portfolio out. Make sure you have help editing the résumé and cover letter, as well as the images.

4. Not understanding the needs and interests of the employer.

Do not forget that grammar and accuracy still count as important characteristics of a cover letter and résumé. A poorly written letter or résumé will often send the wrong message to a potential employer. Editing should be a priority. Make sure to write in short, concise sentences without excess verbiage, and limit the number of

---

CASE STUDY: DENNIS DUNLEAVY

adverbs used to describe your talents. In addition, be sure to personalize your cover letter to address the employer's needs. Sending out a million form letters and résumés is a waste of money and time.

Here are his suggestions for the five most important things to consider on a portfolio:

1. Organization

2. Showing only your best

3. Demonstrating depth and flexibility

4. Clean presentation

5. Experience

Dunleavy reminds job hunters that all the same rules apply to a digital portfolio as they do to print, but you need to be sure the platform will work flawlessly. Make sure your portfolio works on both Macs and PCs. Do not expect a potential employer to go out of the way to make a portfolio work. It should be easy to navigate through and demonstrate your knowledge of the digital world we live in.

IMAGES THAT CAN HURT A PORTFOLIO

It is important to look at each of your portfolio pieces and decide why they should be included. Each piece needs to be your best and needs to be relevant to the purpose behind the portfolio.

Dennis Dunleavy, a college professor teaching visual journalism, has some advice about images that can hurt your portfolio.

He suggests that the images/pictures/samples that you send need to show your work for the resourceful person that you are. According to him, the words and images that work in a résumé and a portfolio are ones that "show" and not "tell" your viewer about your strengths, qualities, and attributes.

He has created a list of images that can hurt your portfolio, and they include:

- Ambiguous meaning
- Confusing center of impact

- Lack of focus
- Stereotypes
- Images without intensity
- Poor technique
- Images without immediacy
- Inability to tell story with one frame
- Context-driver images over impact-drive images
- Assuming the viewer sees what you see

- Clichés
- Missing the moment
- Poor composition
- Images without intimacy

For Dunleavy, the power of an image is in its ability to communicate universal human meaning with immediacy, intensity, and intimacy.

TEACHER'S PORTFOLIO

A portfolio is a key part of your teaching arsenal. They are almost a universal requirement for the job seeker. However, even if you have a secure job, an up-to-date portfolio is a smart thing to have in our uncertain economy.

A teaching portfolio is an expanded résumé that would include a 3-ring binder. This binder is your chance to highlight your strengths, goals, skills, and achievements. Look at it as a serious representation of your professional and teaching abilities.

There are several different elements to consider adding:

- Table of contents
- References
- Transcripts
- Personal goals

- A current résumé
- Letters of recommendation
- Your philosophy on education

- Your classroom management theory

- Teaching tools you have created

- Samples of lessons, units, or special projects

- Information about field trips you may have organized

- Samples of student work

- Photos of you with your students, either in class or on field trips

- Screenshots or URLs of school Web sites you have created

Here are some tips to help create the ultimate teaching portfolio:

- **Make it simple** — This is something that applies to every aspect of job hunting. Do not overload your portfolio with unnecessary text and pictures.

- **Make it manageable** — Three-ring binders are the preferred choice in today's competitive market.

- **Keep it current** — Review it regularly, add to it, and update it as you go. Summer holidays are a perfect time to take a fresh look at the portfolio.

- **Use copies** — Keep the originals and make copies for your portfolio. Consider putting the pictures and captions together on one sheet and then printing off quality color copies for the portfolio.

- **Type the text** — Use the computer whenever possible to type and print out the information.

- **Label** — Use a custom cover to identify your portfolio and consider using page holders on the inside.

THE DESIGN–TECH PORTFOLIO

A design–tech portfolio is similar to other portfolios in that it features parts and pieces of your work. In the case of designers or technicians, it should also deal with concepts, problem solving, and the materials that were important and unique to different projects. It should show the artistry, style, special skills, and individual style of a designer or technician.

Any problem-solving abilities can be featured prominently, particularly if they led to unique design solutions.

A storyboard system works well to show the history, growth, and diversity of skills. With this system:

- You need to edit materials and organize the layout to best feature the work.

- Each page of this type of portfolio tells the story of one project.

- You need to show the skills and styles of the designer.

- If designing clothing, consider putting in a small swatch of the material, show the designs, and show the finished project.

- Include a list of the challenges and then your solutions to these problems.

- Use a solid background board to mount the pictures and the captions or text.

A technical portfolio is similar to a design portfolio in that it tells a story of a project with a focus on the technical aspects. It is important to include a wide range of elements, including technical drawings, budget, engineering solutions, or processes used. The goal with this type of portfolio is to feature the special skills and accomplishments of the technician.

CHAPTER 15:

RÉSUMÉ WRITING SERVICES

The big question as to whether you should use a professional résumé writer to create your résumé is a controversial one. Both sides of this issue have a good point.

Pros

- It is hard to write your résumé objectively

- The job seeker does not always focus on the right issues

- Some job seekers have trouble promoting themselves

- Error-free copy

Cons

- Your résumé might not sound like you

- Your résumé might give an overblown impression of you, which can leave an interviewer feeling deceived when he or she meets you

- Your résumé might present accomplishments in a light that you cannot respond to naturally

- There is a cost involved

The purpose of writing an excellent résumé is to get a job interview. However, do not be so focused on this one step that you forget that the real goal here is to get a good job.

TIME TO USE A RÉSUMÉ WRITING SERVICE

Although most of us, if given enough time and resources, are capable of writing a good résumé, in some circumstances, it is better if we have professional help. Consider using a professional writing service in these circumstances:

- If you have never written a résumé before

- If English is not your first language

- If you need a résumé fast and will not have the time to do it properly

- If you have blights on your record that need to be addressed

- If you have a work history that does not conform to the standard: big gaps, having been fired, or a criminal record

- If you have been out of the job market for an extended time

- If you have not written a résumé for many years and are unsure about the changes required for today's job market

HOW TO FIND A PROFESSIONAL RÉSUMÉ WRITER

If you have all the information and a basic résumé, you might only need to have it typed up into the proper format. Not only is this much cheaper, but it still leaves your personality stamped on the résumé.

If, however, you need someone to create the résumé for you, then it is important to find someone who will give you what you need.

Here are some ways to find a good writer:

- Get a referral from a pleased customer

- Ask potential company if you may speak to previous clients.

- Go to a career center, employment agent, or recruiter and ask for a referral from them.

- Ask your human resources department for referrals if you are being laid off.

- Go through a licensed association, such as the National Résumé Writers' Association (**www.nrwa.com**) or the Professional Association of Résumé Writers and Career Coaches (**www.parw.com**).

HOW TO CHOOSE A PROFESSIONAL RÉSUMÉ WRITER

It is important to find a résumé writer you can talk to. Make sure you are comfortable with the relationship and the arrangement before you hire the writer. This trust will lead to a better working relationship that will in turn help to produce a better résumé for you.

Criteria to consider before choosing a professional writer:

- Make sure you can speak to the writer who will actually be writing your résumé and not someone who will be subcontracting.

- Find out how they are going to gather the required information. Are you going to be interviewed or will you fill in an online form? If it is only a form, then your own words will come back reworded. The form is fine as a place to start, but it is not enough. It is best to be interviewed, allowing more information to come than you might think of on your own. A good résumé writer will know how to find your accomplishments and present them in the best light.

- Find out if your résumé is going to be created from the beginning or if your old one is only being revamped.

- Will you have a chance to make changes after the first draft is finished? You can count on changes being required so make this a condition of the contract.

- How long will it take to get the completed résumé? Consider that a turnaround time of one to two weeks is normal.

- Find out whether you will be meeting with the writer personally. Do they have an office? How will you receive the documents: e-mail, fax, courier, or pick-up?

- How much will the service cost? Fees will vary from less than a hundred dollars to many thousands, depending on your years of experience, number of jobs, and position level, as well as the writer's name and experience. Do not pay per page and ask what additional targeted résumés would cost. If you want to target in several directions, get a bulk price.

- Consider what other services the professional résumé writer offers. They might also write cover letters, distribute your résumé to recruiters, help you with your portfolio, and even offer training and assistance for the interview process.

- Consider using a certified writer. This will not necessarily guarantee you a better résumé than one from a noncertified writer; however, it does guarantee you that the writer has attained a certain standard in the industry.

- Find out if they are willing to do a free initial consultation. This is a brief get-to-know-you phone call directly with the person who is going to write your résumé.

- Ask to see examples of their work, specific to your industry.

WHAT TO WATCH OUT FOR

It would be nice to think that we could place our trust in the professionals to get the job done right. Unfortunately, this is not always the case. Here are several elements that, if you watch for them, can make all the difference.

- Make sure your finished résumé has substance and is not full of clichés and mistakes.

- All industry résumés are not the same — try to work with a specialist in your industry.

- Do not necessarily listen to the endorsements. Approach all services providers with a healthy dose of skepticism.

- When you get your draft back, ask questions about what they did and why. Do not blindly accept the product without understanding the process.

- There is not necessarily a correlation between quality and price. A higher price does not always mean better.

- Ask for an idea of what your finished résumé will look like. Do not let your résumé look like every other résumé on the job market.

- Consider looking at the professional résumé writer's résumé. See whether they have the qualifications before you sign up.

- Work with a company or professional that has a proven track record.

- Get your price, agreed-on services, and delivery date in writing.

- Read over the final draft before giving your approval.

- Make sure to get an electronic version so you can make copies.

- Find out how much it will cost to update your résumé in one month, or even six months.

- Be aware that anyone can call themselves a professional résumé writer — that does not make it so.

- HR credentials are not résumé writing credentials. Do not be fooled into thinking people from this industry will write better résumés than those from other industries. Some will and some will not.

- Make sure your finished résumé is easy to read, with a professionally designed look.

- Make sure there is a profile/highlight section at the top of your résumé. If there is not, question the logic behind this and make sure you agree with it.

- Advance payment is normal, but do not work with any company who wants a nonrefundable deposit or full prepayment. You should not be at risk here.

- Make sure the writer is catering to your industry and not you. You are not hiring, the industry is.

- If you choose to use a professional résumé writer, make sure you get an agreement in writing that the service will not sell or share your résumé with any third parties. Also, check out how the company handles and stores your résumé. They should have a privacy policy that you can read.

ONLINE RÉSUMÉ BUILDERS

An online résumé service is a quick and simple place to start. It is not the best solution, but it is not a bad option for some people.

It is a process whereby you put your information into various fields; when done, the builder spits out a complete résumé – as it is programmed to look. The limitation to this type of program is that it cannot be personalized. These programs are designed to benefit the employment side of the industry, not the job seeker. These are actually templates, and your final version will need to be amended as needed. For example, if you do not want to put in references, you will have to delete that section.

CHAPTER 16:

TODAY'S JOB MARKET

THE GLOBAL JOB MARKET

The job market today is worldwide. That presents not only exciting opportunities but hidden pitfalls. Words do not mean the same in every country and education does not have the same emphasis depending on where you are looking.

CASE STUDY: MARY ANNE THOMPSON

Mary Anne Thompson is an internationally renowned speaker and author on global employment topics. She is the founder of **www.goinglobal.com**, an informational Web site dedicated to global careers.

With over ten years' experience in her area of specialty, Thompson "accidentally fell" into her current career when she lived overseas and could not continue to practice as a lawyer, due to the local certification issues. She began providing advice for writing a corporate profile for an overseas company. This process forced her to "step back" and rewrite all résumés, understanding their backgrounds. This developed into writing career columns. Her career advice has been featured in numerous publications, both here and overseas.

Since her start in this industry, Thompson has noticed that everyone is "going global — even 'mom and pop' companies are going cross-border." She sees the industry becoming more standardized, moving toward an "all-electronic" structure and an increase in the importance of using keywords.

Over the years, she has recognized the same mistakes showing up repeatedly. Thompson stresses the importance of using your contacts and networking to find the right job for you. She offers this advice: "Put yourself in [the] reader's shoes and include info of interest that is targeted to that particular reader/job opening."

In her list of the worst things to do in an application package, she puts typos at the top. She believes that typos or a "sloppy" résumé translates to a "sloppy" employee.

CASE STUDY: MARY ANNE THOMPSON

She also considers it a mistake to make a résumé too general or not targeted for a particular position. She also recommends including specific accomplishments and "quantifying" accomplishments wherever possible. One mistake she recommends you do not make is to leave a critical piece of experience or information out of your résumé in hopes that you can add this as "new" information in an interview.

She offers the following points to make the most of your résumé:

1. Spell check repeatedly and get another person to proofread.

2. Target the résumé to a particular job.

3. Quantify/specify all accomplishments.

4. Have a strong, multifaceted qualification summary at beginning of the résumé in a bullet point format.

5. Make sure résumé is "culturally" correct — have a "local" review the content.

As she sees greater interest in candidates who are bilingual and have multicultural experience, here is her advice to the job seeker of today: "Take calculated risks that may lead to better job experience, and do not forget to learn a second language."

The following article is reprinted with permission from Mary Anne Thompson. For additional information, please visit **www.goinglobal.com.**

HOW TO CREATE A GLOBAL RÉSUMÉ/CV

By Mary Anne Thompson, Founder, **www.goinglobal.com**

Interest among both new and seasoned professionals in pursuing international careers has skyrocketed in recent years. Such interest has been enhanced by chronic personnel shortages in home markets that are causing companies to actively search beyond their borders for talent.

Professionals of all ages are proactively seeking career experiences outside their home countries for a variety of professional and personal reasons — the need to recharge their batteries with a new challenge, the opportunity to have a position with more responsibility that encourages creativity and initiative (and typically involves a promotion to boot!), the wish to expose their children to another culture and the opportunity to learn a second language, and the recognition that many of those who have "climbed to the top" of the corporate ladder have leap-frogged ahead after a global work experience.

Résumé/CV guidelines are in a constant state of change. There are no hard-and-fast rules that are 100 percent appropriate in every case. The best advice is to do

CASE STUDY: MARY ANNE THOMPSON

your homework — find out what is appropriate vis-a-vis the corporate culture, the country culture, and the culture of the person making the hiring decision. The challenge will be to incorporate several different cultures into one document.

Some general advice:

- The terms "résumé" and "CV" (curriculum vitae) generally mean the same thing the world over, i.e., a document describing one's educational and professional experience that is prepared for job-hunting purposes. When there is a difference, a CV is typically a lengthier version of a résumé, complete with numerous attachments. Note: The average length for a résumé or CV is two pages — no matter the country, no matter the position. Never ever try to "get around the rules" by shrinking your font size to an unreadable level or printing your résumé on the front and back sides of one piece of paper. Neither is an acceptable technique under any circumstance. Never "stretch" your résumé to two pages but also never "sell yourself short" by limiting yourself to one page.

- Different countries use different terms to describe the specific aspects of what a résumé/CV should contain. For example, "cover letters" are called "letters of interest" in some countries and "motivation letters" in others. Another example… photographs are not appropriate to be attached to résumés in the United States; and if one is attached anyway, the employer is required to dispose of it. In many countries outside the United States, it is standard procedure to attach a photo or have your photo printed on your CV. Also, some countries require original copies of transcripts and references to be attached to your application.

- Education requirements differ country to country. In almost every case of "cross-border" job hunting, merely stating the title of your degree would not necessarily be an adequate description. The reader still might not have a clear understanding of what topics you studied or for how many years (i.e., in some countries, a university degree can be obtained in three years and in othecountries it takes five years to receive a degree). If you are a recent graduate, and depending heavily on your educational background to get a job, provide the reader with details about your studies and any related projects/ experience. The same advice is true for seasoned professionals who have participated in numerous training or continuous education courses — provide the reader with specific information on what you learned, the number of course hours, and so on. Note: The general rule is that your university training strictly becomes "a line item" on your résumé (i.e., no further details needed) once you have five or more years of professional experience.

If you have specific training, education or expertise, use industry-accepted

CASE STUDY: MARY ANNE THOMPSON

terminology in your description. Use language and terms that any professional in your field would understand, no matter where in the world he/she lives.

- Pay particular attention whether to write your résumé in chronological or reverse-chronological order. Chronological order means: start by listing your first or "oldest" work experience. Reverse-chronological order means: start by listing your current or most recent experience first. Most countries have definite preferences about which format is most acceptable. If there are no specific guidelines given, the general preference is that a résumé/CV be written in a reverse-chronological format.

- The level of computer technology and accessibility to the Internet varies widely country to country. Even if a company or individual lists an e-mail address, there is no guarantee that they actually received your mail. Always make sure to e-mail your résumé as an attachment and in a widely accepted format, such as MS Word. I would always recommend sending a hard copy of your résumé/CV via "snail mail" just to make sure that it is received.

- Computer skills and language skills are always important, no matter the job, no matter the country. Take care to describe your skill levels in detail in both categories.

- If you are submitting your résumé in English, find out if the recipient uses "British" English or "American" English. There are numerous variations between the two versions. A reader who is unfamiliar with the variations just présumés that the résumé contains typos.

  Most European companies use "British" English though most United States companies — no matter where they are based in the world — use "American" English. Almost every computer today provides you with both options.

- Spell check, spell check, spell check, then get a human being to spell check your résumé/CV. Incorrectly spelled words or typos are frowned upon by human resource professionals the world over. The presumption is that if you submit a sloppy, careless résumé, you will be a sloppy, careless worker. A human "spell checker" is especially valuable for catching words that are spelled properly but are used incorrectly. The same is true for taking the time to double-check the correct title, gender and spelling of the name of the recipient of your résumé. In the United States, "Jan" is a woman's name though it is a man's name in Europe.

- If you can, get someone who is a native speaker of the language in which your résumé/CV is written to review your document. Résumés/CV's written by non-native language speakers tend to include terms, though correct in the exac translation, that are never used on an everyday basis. For example, several

CASE STUDY: MARY ANNE THOMPSON

foreign résumés/CVs submitted to U.S. employers describe university/college education as "tertiary" education. Although "tertiary" is literally correct, it is a term that is almost never used in the United States. One goal of your résumé/CV is to show your familiarity with the culture by using culturally appropriate language. Anything else just highlights that you may not be a candidate who can "hit the ground running."

- Be aware that stationery or paper sizes are different dimensions in different countries. The United States standard is 8½ x 11 inches whereas the European A-4 standard is 210 x 297 mm. When you are transmitting your résumé/CV via e-mail, go to "page setup" on your computer and reformat your document to the recipient's standard. Otherwise, when they print it out on their end, half of your material will be missing! The same is true for sending a fax. If you transmit material typed on "irregular" size paper, half of it will be missing on the other end. If at all possible, purchase stationery that has the same dimensions as the recipient's and mail/fax your résumé on that stationery.

- Most multinational companies will expect you to speak both the language of that country and English, which is widely accepted today as being the universal language of business. Have your résumé/CV drafted in both languages and be prepared for your interview to be conducted in both languages. Most companies want to "see" and "hear" actual proof of your language skills early in the hiring process.

- The safest way to ensure that your document is "culturally correct" is to review as many examples as possible. Ask the employer or recruiter for examples of résumés that they thought were particularly good.

- Work permit and visa regulations appear very similar country to country. In very general terms, most employers who want to hire "foreigners," "aliens" or "expatriates" must be able to certify to the government that they were unable to find locals with the required skill sets. The fastest way to be hired abroad is either to actively seek a country where there is a shortage of people with your skills (IT backgrounds are pretty "hot" everywhere) or to be an "intra-company" transfer from another country. Be aware that obtaining a work permit can take many, many months.

- Lastly, to be successful and enjoy your experience abroad, you must be flexible and open-minded, both eager and willing to learn new ways of doing things. You must be willing to "When in Rome, do as the Romans do." To hold fast to your own cultural traditions even when they offend another or render you ineffective is a waste of everyone's time. People everywhere appreciate individuals who are at least interested in getting to know them and learn about their ways of doing

CASE STUDY: MARY ANNE THOMPSON

things. Enormous cultural faux pas are forgiven of pleasant individuals who are making honest attempts to fit in. On the other hand, arrogant know-it-alls can sink million-dollar deals just by their boisterous attitudes. Be patient and observant. Ask questions; show your interest in learning and broadening your horizons.

Be aware that you represent your country to everyone you meet. You may be the first Australian that a German has ever met. Both of these individuals will walk away from the initial encounter assuming that all Australians or all Germans are just like you. Representing an entire country is a major responsibility and one that you should be aware of in everything you say and do.

So, go out and give the world a twirl. Here are the tools; the rest is up to you!

For particular information about a country's requirements, check out Thompson's Web site, **Goingglobal.com**.

CLEANING UP YOUR ONLINE PRESENCE

Few people think of the negative impact of participating online. We are not talking about your published articles and Web site here. Although those do count, this is more about blogs and what other people might be saying about you. Today, it can be difficult to tell what other people, even your friends, are saying about you online. If you post or reply to someone's blog, your name is shown for all to see. The blog you wrote can be picked up and commented on by someone else. They might or might not have understood what you were saying, but you will have no control over what they say about you and your writing. Once you have written something down on the Internet, you lose control of it, people can quote, twist, and respond in any way they like, using your name at all times.

This can be very bad for you and your reputation.

Start by typing your name, and all common variations of your name, into a main search engine, like **google.com** (or **Yahoo.com**, or **MSN.com**) and see what comes up. Sometimes the results are shocking. The material you wrote ten years ago as a teenager with attitude is probably still out there. Even worse, there is no way for the recruiters of today to know you were only 14 at the time.

Can you see the problem? A high percentage of recruiters and hiring managers check online for the names of viable candidates, just to see what comes up. How can anyone not be influenced by what they find?

So, because search engines are only going to get more tenacious, here are some tips suggested by Jared Flesher in his article, "How to Clean Up Your Digital Dirt Before It Trashes Your Job Search":

1. If you belong to an online community like Facebook, make sure all information you have listed is how you would want a recruiter to see it. You can also change your settings so that only friends and other students can view your information.

2. Clean up your "digital dirt," or unflattering personal information. One possible way to cover up this type of online information is to make the pages you want recruiters to see have more links to them than there are to the pages you do not want them to see. Basically, overwhelm the bad news with good news. The search engines rank their results based on the number of sites that link to those pages, so you need to increase the number of links to the good pages. According to Luis Villa, a senior technology analyst at the Berkman Center for Internet and Society at Harvard Law School, "The best way to make something bad go away is to have a lot of web presence, such as starting a web page or a blog of your own."

3. Another suggestion is to monitor what is being said about you through a site like **Pubsub.com**. This site will alert you by e-mail if your name is mentioned in any Internet newsgroups, blogs, or securities filings. The site is based in New York. Salim Ismail, the chief executive officer and cofounder of the site, explains it this way, "It is as if you put a filter on a hose and catch the information as it goes by, allowing them to select out the relevant material they want to know about." It is useful, particularly for people who have a reason to keep track of what people are saying.

ELECTRONIC FORMS

In many cases, your hard-earned, finished product is unused in the first stage of job hunting. Many large companies are converting to online application forms, where each job hunter fills out certain fields designed to cover the basics of their résumé. These can be awkward and time consuming, as well as very restrictive. There is usually a box to put in additional comments; however, the flow and focus of the résumé has become chopped up, and it is hard to recapture the same message.

Many of these application forms include the fill-in fields as well as a field for you to cut and paste in your cover letter and résumé. These two items have to be in an electronic format. Therefore, if you have only a standard copy, you need to take the time to create the electronic version before you start these online applications.

Once you have completed the application form, you will be sent a confirmation e-mail. Some of these online application systems will assign you a user ID number. This allows you to log in again, so you can go and update or change your application.

This type of system allows you to go in and apply as new jobs come up without having to refill in the forms. You can use your ID number to apply and your saved information is automatically pulled. That is why it is so important to update your résumé on these places.

In some cases, these systems are set up so you can also see the status of jobs that you have applied for. This allows you to see if the job is still open, if they are screening the applicants, if they have made it to the interview stage, or if the position is now filled.

IDENTITY THEFT AND THE JOB SEARCH

Most job hunters never think about the security risks of spreading their résumé everywhere. It is necessary in today's job hunting world to circulate your résumé when looking for work. Unfortunately, there are criminals who are delighted with this trend. After all, your résumé has "street value," as Pam Dixon, founder and executive director of the World Privacy Forum, puts it. Your name, address, telephone details, and work history are prized by identity thieves and other criminals.

It is important to learn where and when you can post your résumé to protect it against those who would make a profit from you.

Dixon offers the following truths about posting your résumé online:

- **Post your résumé "privately."** There are job sites that allow you to post online without showing your contact information or e-mail address. This type of option gives you the chance to control who can contact you. If you choose to post your résumé without this option, do not put down your full address or phone number, and use an e-mail you can cancel if problems arise down the road.

- **Once downloaded, your résumé can be used in many different ways, and many of them are not good.** The job seeker needs to beware.

- **More than recruiters are looking at job site databases.** It is common practice for private investigators and law firms to use résumé databases of well-known job sites to find people.

- **Never put a social security number on your résumé.** Do not e-mail it to a prospective employer either. A real employer will not ask for it until you are hired, usually after several interviews.

- **All job sites are not equal. Before posting your résumé online, find the privacy policy of the site and question the owner if you need to.** If there are no privacy policies posted, that should be a warning in itself. Also, if you cannot delete it when you need to, do not post it in the first place. Look to see how long the site will store your résumé until the site deletes it. You do not want your résumé circulating for years after you have gotten a wonderful job.

- **Do not post references.** You would be posting personal information on these people that could cause them many problems.

- **Some posted jobs are scams.** Fake jobs have become a real issue. If you are asked to scan in and send your ID or driver's license, do not do it. The more general a job description is, the more likely it is to be fake. Some jobs are just trying to get you to post your résumé on a new site.

- **Some job sites are better than other job sites.** According to Dixon, it is important to be aware that some sites will sell your résumé to another site, and some steal résumés to post on their sites.

- **Keep records of where you have posted your résumé.** If you apply with an online form, print off a copy so you have a record. These will help you to follow up later.

- **Prevention is the safest answer.** If you believe your personal information has been shared or used in any way, there is very little you can do about it after the fact. It is better to be safe and act responsibly in the first place.

Pam Dixon suggests checking out **http://www.worldprivacyforum.org/ jobscamtipspayforwarding.html** for information about avoiding job scams.

ONLINE SEARCHES AND PRIVACY

One of the concerns about the Internet is the vast amount of information that is available. Wrong information, old information, or private information can be a problem. There have always been ways to search out information on people. Hiring private investigators was the standard method for years. Now there are companies that specialize in online services for looking up information.

These directory companies offer people-search services that are very comprehensive and reasonably priced. They can find details, maybe true and maybe not, about anyone online. This is a scary opportunity that can be exploited by identity thieves or other criminals.

Companies are adamant that they are only searching for information that has already been made public.

According to an article by Jessica E. Vascellaro, **Wink.com** says that they do not use information designated "private" by such sites as MySpace. This company searches over 150 million profiles to find people by name, facts, and screen name in their profiles, location, and interests. Expansion is planned to be able to search for people among blogs, Web pages, and photos.

Some of these companies, like **ZoomInfo.com**, allow you to go in and add additional work history and pictures, as well as remove incorrect data. This company searches Web pages, press releases, and other sources for information. They actively encourage people to log in, verify their identities, and make the necessary changes. To remove data, you have to prove that the information is incorrect. However, it is an excellent way to see what is floating around on the Internet that you might not know about, but that a recruiter or hiring manager might.

One of the negative side effects of this type of service is that they cannot sort through the large amount of misinformation and inaccuracies from sources like social networks and blogs. Some of the material is false; there is duplicate material and some very out-of-date material. The search does not have the ability to weed though the information the way you might need it to. Consider the problems of people with the same name.

CHAPTER 17:
THE BASICS FOR THE JOB INTERVIEW

It is hard to imagine anything more nerve-wracking than a job interview. Chances are you have been laid off, fired, or have been out of work for a while, and this job interview is important. That means you have to prepare — practice your questions and be confident.

Some general basics that need to be followed are:

- Do not smoke, eat, or chew gum immediately prior to the job interview

- Dress properly

- Do your wage research before going

- Be on time

- Take a clean copy of your résumé or CV with you

- Greet the interviewer by name

- Use a good, firm handshake

- Do not sit down until invited to do so

- Stay focused on the interviewer and what he or she is saying

- Act professional

- Show a sense of humor

- Be enthusiastic and interested

- Answer questions clearly and succinctly

- Do not avoid a question

- Do not get into discussions about politics or religion

- Do not, under any circumstances, complain about any current or former employer

- Do not open discussions about wages

- Avoid making the interview all about you

Start your interview with a simple greeting. How you answer the initial opening statements, called "ice breakers," is important.

Sometimes, the interviewer will ask how you are doing, or if you had any difficulty finding the place. They are not asking because they really want to know, they are asking to see how you answer. Therefore, keep your answers brief and polite. Do not reply using words like:

- Okay

- Not so well

- It was all right

- So-so

- Whatever

THE BASICS OF FIRST IMPRESSIONS

BEING ON TIME

Take the few minutes required to look up where the interview is being held. Either find transit information to get to your interview or look up driving instructions. If you have time, consider going there to find the place before the interview, or leave enough time in case you get lost or cannot find parking.

Bring enough coins if meters are the only type of parking available to you.

You do not want to be early, and you are never to be late. Arriving five minutes ahead of the scheduled time is fine.

Do not have another appointment to go to. You never walk out of an interview because you are pressed for time. Schedule your day appropriately. An interview can last from five minutes to a half-day. You can phone ahead of time and ask how long the interview is scheduled for. Better yet, clear your day and be prepared for anything.

Refer to the end of this chapter for an idea of the different types of interviews.

DRESSING PROPERLY

The initial impression is based on several things, but your appearance accounts for close to half of this perception. Therefore, dressing appropriately is important.

Much research has been done on what to wear for a job interview. There are tips to help you, but they will not be applicable to every situation. Some industries are case specific. If you do not know, feel free to phone the company and ask the receptionist or a human resources assistant. Do not ask the human resources manager.

- Dress conservatively. Even if the other staff members are dressed casually, it is important to show up for the first interview in conservative, professional attire.

- Be well groomed with a neat and tidy hairstyle.

- For women with long hair, it is suggested that you have your hair up, or at least pinned back so you are not constantly tossing your hair or moving locks behind your ears.

- Have clean, trimmed fingernails with no-color to pale-colored nail polish.

- If you are going to use cologne or perfume, keep it to a minimum. These scents create havoc with people's allergies, and you do not want to set off any that your interviewer might have.

- Wear minimal jewelry.

- Wear minimal body piercings — it is better to have no visible body piercings.

Especially for women:

- Wear shoes with conservative heels

- Use minimal make-up

- Minimal jewelry — one ring and one set of earrings

- Avoid dresses

Especially for men:

- Wear a conservative suit — two piece suit and tie, in a solid color.

- Wear a long-sleeve shirt.

- Wear dark shoes and dark socks.

- Be clean-shaven if possible. Keep facial hair well trimmed.

- Have a short, conservative haircut.

- Avoid a beard.

- Do not wear jewelry, other than a single ring.

EMOTIONALLY AND MENTALLY READY

BODY LANGUAGE

A simple understanding of body language will help you to maximize yours during an interview. Knowing our weaknesses means we can learn to turn them into strengths.

- **Handshake** — A firm, dry handshake is important. It shows a strong, confident personality. A limp, sweaty handshake is what you do not want to have. The handshake is one of the first body language signs that the interviewer will be looking to understand.

- **Hands** — Do not wave them around or gesture wildly while trying to make a point. Move your hands a little, otherwise, keep them in your lap.

- **Eye contact** — Keep eye contact with the interviewer. Do not stare and do not look out the window. It is important for them to feel like you are interested and paying attention.

- **Posture** — This is important, as it shows your attitude. Standing or sitting properly shows energy, enthusiasm, and interest. Slouching reflects a poor attitude.

- **Fidgeting** — Do not play with your hair, bang your fingers on the chair or desk, or display any other mannerism that might show that you are nervous or impatient.

WHAT TO RESEARCH BEFORE THE INTERVIEW

Researching the company is just common sense. It allows you to have a better understanding of the company, how it operates, what it does, and how it does it. It will also help you to create a list of the basic things you would like to know.

Research and preparation for the job interview will help you to understand:

- Hiring procedures
- Corporate culture
- The company organization
- Your potential supervisor

- The hiring process
- The company history
- The corporate structure
- The size of the organization
- The number of employees
- The location(s) of the company
- The job description of the open position
- What type of business the company is involved in
- The various career elements of the company
- The culture within the company
- The location of the interview
- The industry the company is in
- The type and names of competitors
- How long the company has been in business
- General knowledge of the industry
- The way the company operates

WHERE TO RESEARCH

Besides researching the company so that you can ask a couple of intelligent questions and understand the way the company works, it is important to understand the wages. Do your wage research to be in a strong bargaining position. If you have no idea what other people in similar jobs are making, how can you tell if what they are offering is fair?

Places to look for some valuable information include:

- The public library
- Local bookstores
- Magazines
- Journals

- Newspapers
- Reference books

Some companies offer investor packs, which contain valuable information for the job seeker. The main competitors to the company are also great sources for information.

When looking for research material, do not forget to consider the people in your world. Your network of business contacts, friends, and family can be a great source of information.

CVtips.com offers the following online sources to help you find what you need. Consider:

- **www.BizJournals.com**
- **www.valueline.com**
- **www.LexisNexis.com**

There are excellent Web sites for major business publications as well. Here are a few of the better-known sites.

- **www.kiplinger.com**
- **www.investors.com**
- **www.forbes.com**
- **www.money.cnn.com**
- **www.wsj.com**

WAGE RESEARCH

You want to be in the best negotiating position possible when it comes time to talk about salary. To be in a strength position, you have to do your research. You should know as much as possible about:

- The general economic situation
- The company's situation in the industry
- The unemployment rate in the industry

- The qualifications and experience that could be expected for this position

- The company bottom line in terms of profits

- The pay scale within the company

- The company organization

- The age of the company

- The developmental maturity of the company

The following are points where you are bargaining from:

- Other vacancies of a similar level

- You unique skill set and experience

- How long you can afford to be out of work

- How heavy the competition is

The interviewer is bargaining from these points:

- How important the position is for the company

- How quickly the position needs to be filled

- How tight the budget constraints are

- Who set the salary for the position

Knowing each other's position can help you to negotiate your career salary.

QUESTIONS TO CONSIDER ASKING

Toward the end of the interview, you will be given an opportunity to ask questions. It is always a good idea to have one or two questions prepared. This is also the time to clarify any information that might have been brought up during the interview that you did not understand.

Not asking questions may give the impression that you were:

- Not prepared
- Not listening
- Not interested

This question period is a great opportunity to show your newly acquired knowledge of the current industry situation. Do not overdo the questions. The questions to ask will depend on the position you applying for, the situation, and your relationship with the interviewer(s).

Some typical questions to consider asking include:

1. Do you have a job description for this position?

2. What type of software does the company use?

3. Can you tell me more about the structure of the organization?

4. How do you evaluate performances in the company?

5. What are the skills you consider the most important for this job?

Asking questions during an interview not only shows that you have been paying attention and did your research, it also helps to establish a rapport with the interviewer.

INTERVIEW QUESTIONS

An interview is a test. How you answer the questions will be judged with a tally at the end of the interview as to whether you are still a viable candidate or not. The way to pass this test with excellence is to practice.

First practice alone and then in front of friends, family members, and career counselors. It also helps if you can be taped and see how you appear to others. Once you have practiced, identify areas that need improvement and practice again. Then look to your résumé and CV and identify weaknesses. Think about potential questions that an employer could ask, and practice answering them. Look at your body posture and see if you need to improve your body language. Then practice again.

There are going to be various types of questions. There will be general questions about you, your goals, your past work experience, and your résumé; then there will be questions called behavioral interview questions.

Here are some things to think about before you answer:

- The job and the employer's needs coming first

- How the answer will help you to achieve the company's goals

- How you can contribute

- Being specific

- Being clear

- Giving examples

- Not rambling or mumbling

- Using your accomplishments as examples

- Explaining why you did something as well as you did it

- If you do not understand the question, ask for clarification

- Speak slowly and directly to the interviewer

GENERAL QUESTIONS

The more general questions could include any or all of the following:

1. What made you apply to this company?

2. Why are you interested in this industry?

3. What made you go into this field?

4. Why are you interested in this job?

5. Why do you think you are the right person for this position?

6. What qualities do you think are required to excel at this job?

7. What do you know about this company?

8. Why do you want to work for the company?

9. Do you have any questions about the company?

10. What do you consider your ideal job?

11. How long have you been looking for a new job?

12. What are you looking for in your next job?

13. What do you feel are your best contributions to your next job?

14. Why are you looking to change your job?

15. What do you think this job will offer you that your current one does not?

16. What were your contributions to your current company?

17. What were your contributions to your last company?

18. What types of jobs are you looking at right now?

19. How could you improve your current position?

20. How could you improve yourself?

21. What is your greatest accomplishment?

22. What is your greatest failure?

23. How are you at handling criticism?

24. How well do you work as part of a team?

25. How well do you work on your own?

26. How well do you evaluate your effort and work?

27. What problems did you encounter in your last job?

28. How did you overcome these problems?

29. What are you greatest motivators?

30. Are you competitive?

31. How did your previous jobs make you the ideal person for this position?

32. Are you ready for more responsibility?

33. Would you consider yourself easy to work with?

34. How do you handle working under pressure?

35. Are you dependable?

36. Do you pride yourself on completing a job well done?

37. Do you consider yourself successful?

38. How do you see yourself making a difference in this company?

39. How did you progress in your last company?

40. Why should we hire you?

These are just simple examples. The questions can be more pointed and more direct. If you have not practiced, then they can throw you off and make it hard to answer naturally.

BEHAVIORAL QUESTIONS

Behavioral questions are when an interviewer will ask for examples of a time when you had to do something specific. This could be related to a job duty, communication skills, or specific projects, even aggressive marketing tactics you have employed to bring about a certain result. The interviewers are looking for certain skills like multitasking, patience, strategy, flexibility, diplomacy, and marketing tactics. This technique is great to see how fast you can react, how quickly you think on your feet, and how well you can pull from your experience to handle critical issues.

The best way to deal with these types of questions is preparation. Before this type of interview, prepare to discuss a few highlights and low times that you dealt with successfully to help you answer the type of questions that will be asked. Think about how you might have handled a difficult client or solved a disaster before a deadline, or an emergency you might have been involved in. Try to relate these points to the new position you are applying for. For example, if diplomacy is required, pull from your history a time when your diplomacy won the day.

The interviewer is looking to see how you managed to solve these types of situations in a way that benefited the company. Give the details and do not be shy. Do not exaggerate, because they may check with your references. These detailed answers could get you the job.

Even though you have prepared for this type of interview, you might still be caught with unexpected questions. You cannot anticipate every angle. If this happens, try to improvise. Answer the question honestly and to the best of your ability. If you have never had the type of experience that the interviewer is asking for, say so and then explain how you would handle this type of situation if it had happened.

There has been a trend over the last decade toward asking behavioral questions during an interview. If you have never seen these types of questions before, they can be disconcerting to answer without preparation. There are many questions like these, but here are some of the more common for you to think about. Read them over and try to find a reasonable answer with examples to back it up.

1. Can you describe a time when you were faced with a problem or a particularly stressful situation at work that tested your ability to cope? How did you handle this situation?

2. Please give an example of when you had to make a quick decision that mattered to the company. Was it the right decision?

3. Give an example of when you went above the call of duty for your job.

4. Can you describe a time when other people in the company depended on you?

5. Describe a problem you have had with a coworker. How did you handle the situation?

6. Can you describe an instance when you had to tell other people what you thought?

7. Explain a situation when you did not have the skills to do a job asked of you. How did you handle it?

8. Give an example of when you had to use your communication skills to get a point across to make something happen.

9. Can you explain how you set goals and attain them? Please give an example.

10. What has been the highlight of your career? Why?

11. What was the most important presentation or document that you have created? Why?

12. Please describe a situation when you were able to build motivation with your coworkers.

13. Give an example of when you could not finish a task because you did not have enough information. How did you handle it?

14. Describe a situation when you were required to deal with an upset customer, client, or employee.

15. What is the worst situation you have had to deal with in your job in the past couple of years?

16. Please describe a situation when you disagreed with company policy, but followed it anyway.

17. Explain a team project that you were involved in and your role on the team.

18. Tell me about the worst coworker or supervisor you have had and explain why. How did you handle working with this person?

19. Give an example of when you were able to communicate with another, even if you did not like them or they did not like you.

20. Can you describe a situation when your quick thinking saved the day?

21. Give an example of how you were effective in your previous job.

22. Can you explain a situation where you were required to put organization in place to make something happen?

23. Can you explain a difficult situation with a client and how you handled it?

24. Can you describe an emergency and how you handled it?

25. What is the most creative work project you have been a part of?

26. Can you describe a situation when you had to deal with another

employee doing something illegal or wrong within the company? What did you do about it?

27. Can you describe a project that you worked on for the company that helped other people less fortunate? What was your role in this project?

28. Explain a time when you wished you were no longer in this industry. What made you decide to stay?

29. Explain a time when you changed your actions based on another person's values at work.

30. What would you do if you saw an employee stealing office supplies?

31. Describe a situation in which you influenced another person in a positive direction.

32. Describe a situation that reinforced for you that you are in the right industry.

33. Give an example of when you were inspired to do better on a project. What inspired you? What were the results?

SALARY NEGOTIATIONS

When you have been offered a job, you are then in the position of deciding whether you are going to accept it or not. In order to make this decision, you need to understand the wages being offered and the benefit package that might accompany the wages. Prior to this stage, you should have done your research (see the section on Wage Research) and should have all the facts in hand so you can decide whether the package is fair.

ASSESSING A JOB OFFER

It is tempting to immediately accept an offer, but you need to assess the offer to make the best decision.

Things to consider are:

- Start date — is it flexible?

- Job title and duties

- Work schedule

- Overtime required?

    a) Is there compensation?

    b) Are there flexible hours?

    c) Is evening and weekend work required?

- Is the job permanent? Temporary? Contract? On-call?

    a) How long is the probation period?

- Are there opportunities to move up or transfer to another area?

    a) How are the employee evaluations handled?

    b) Is the position stable — is it secure?

- Salary and the accompanying package

- Compensation, bonus structure, earning potential

    a) What is the base salary?

    b) How often will you be paid?

    c) Are there commissions or bonuses? If so, how are they calculated?

    d) When are salaries reviewed?

    e) What is included in the benefits package?

- Are there training and professional development opportunities available?

    a) Is on-the-job training provided?

    b) Will the company pay for continuing education?

- Will you have to travel far to work?

    a) Is parking provided?

    b) Are travel expenses covered?

    c) Will the company pay for relocation?

- Do you agree with the working conditions and culture of the company?

- Are you happy about the company's reputation?

- Long-term potential

You can request a meeting to discuss any of the items mentioned above.

NEGOTIATING SALARY AND OTHER DETAILS

Understand that an interviewer will have a range to work with and will generally offer the bottom of the range. It is up to you to negotiate upward. Only accept the first offer if you are very desperate for a job. Try to ask for a little time to think it over.

They may offer the job and a start date, but not mention a salary until you have said yes. They will also ask you what salary you need. Do not answer this question. During these negotiations, make sure you let them know that you are negotiating toward an agreement that is good for both parties. Underline the skills you are bringing to the company and your interest and enthusiasm at joining the company. This is your starting point for the company and one of the easiest times to request a raise.

Do not settle for something less than you want because you are afraid to negotiate. Take the time to learn about salary negotiation and other career techniques. There are a few helpful tips to negotiate an improvement on the offer:

- As mentioned earlier, do your research. Find the salary ranges for similar positions within your industry.

- If the salary is fixed, then consider whether it is possible to get performance bonuses, earlier increases, or other benefits, like working a shorter work week or getting extra vacation time.

- Always be polite.

- Get it in writing — all items discussed and agreed upon need to be included in the written offer.

- Ask for a day or two to think about the offer.

DECLINING A JOB OFFER

If you are going to decline an offer, tell the company as soon as possible. This can be done over the phone or in writing. Make sure to thank them and provide an explanation. Always be professional; you do not know when you might be in contact with the company again.

ACCEPTING A JOB OFFER

You can accept an offer over the telephone, in person, in writing, and even by e-mail. Sometimes you will be asked to sign a letter of employment contract.

Always be polite and professional, and show your appreciation for the offer.

WHAT TO BRING

You do not need much for an interview, but there are a few factors that will make you look more professional and will strengthen your case. Consider being prepared by bringing the following:

- A briefcase (instead of a purse for women)

- A copy of your résumé or CV

- A list of references to hand over if requested

- A salary history, if requested earlier

TYPES OF INTERVIEWS

You may be called to any one of several different types of interviews. Some are specific to the level of position, and some are more industry specific.

ONE-ON-ONE JOB INTERVIEW

The only type of job interview most people will experience is one on one. This is you with one person — the interviewer. This is the typical question-and-answer type of interview where, by the end, the interviewer has some idea whether you are suitable and you have some idea whether you are interested.

The interview starts when the two parties meet. In these first few minutes, the interviewer will have already read various signals, body language, and other nonverbal signals, including the way your are dressed.

The purpose is, of course, for the interviewer to determine whether you are the right person for the job. This will include general questions and technical questions. The general questions are intended to see your problem-solving and teamwork abilities. They are looking to see if you have facts to back up your statements.

As part of the process to see how you fit into the work environment, the team you will be working with, and your supervisor, chances are good that you will need to have several one-on-one interviews. This process can take several days to a week with a nerve-wracking wait in between. Each time you pass one round of interviews, you move up to be interviewed by the person higher up.

Each of these interviews must go very well in order to move up. Each interviewer might not necessarily know what you said to a previous one. You need to sell yourself each time.

PANEL INTERVIEW

This interview is conducted by a panel of interviewers. This group is usually made up of the supervisor and team members. Depending on the type of position you are applying for, the panel could be made up of top-level executive officers.

There is no way to get through this type of interview without some stress. This is why it is used. The company wants to see your reaction to stress. All the members will ask questions, and sometimes the same question in different ways. The setup loses any comfortable relationship-building type of communication. It can also be difficult to connect in any positive way with the members.

The questions can come hard and fast, and it can be difficult to think straight. Asking questions yourself can help break up the pressure. It is important to remain calm during this type of interview. They are looking to see how you handle this type of stress.

GROUP INTERVIEW

This type of interview is probably the worst of all the interview types. It is certainly very stressful. In this instance, all the job candidates will be interviewed at the same time in the same room, as a group.

With this type of interview, the company is looking to see:

- Who are the leaders

- Stress levels of each candidate

- How the candidate faces the situation

- Communication skills in a group setting

- The knowledge level of each person

This type of interview can make it difficult to get equal time while giving the other people a chance to speak. Ignore others that are being aggressive or difficult. This is not usually a final interview. It is often a way to get through many candidates to find those to be short-listed.

PHONE INTERVIEW

A phone interview is usually the first interview. It is used when people live a long way from the location of the position. Regardless of the reason for the interview, the goal is the same — to get a face-to-face interview. You should do your research prior to this type of interview.

Techniques to remember for this type of interview include:

- Be enthusiastic

- Stay focused

- Do not be working on the computer at the same time — your distraction will be noticed

- Turn off any background music

- Remove yourself from family

- Turn off any distractions

- Take notes if you need to

- Remember to ask questions, if you have any

- Consider practicing phone interviews with a friend

- Follow the same rules as for face-to-face interviews

- Do not smoke, drink, or eat during the interview

- Do not discuss salary over the phone

- Ask when it would be convenient for a traditional interview

- Speak slowly and clearly

LUNCH INTERVIEW

This type of interview is longer, as it covers the full time it takes to order and eat a meal at a restaurant. However, this interview still requires the same amount of preparation as the other types.

Your lunch interview is not to evaluate your table manners, although a certain amount are required to pass to the next level; rather, it is your ability to do the job that is being judged.

Having said that, remember to not do these few things:

- Put your elbows on the table

- Slurp noisily

- Be rude to other customers or the staff

- Drink alcohol

- Speak with your mouth full of food

- Sneeze or cough on the food

- Complain about the food

Tips to make this interview as good as can be:

- Do your research first

- Research the restaurant before arriving

- Know what you are going to order

- Order a small, light meal

- Avoid eating strong-smelling foods

- Avoid meals that are messy to eat

- Avoid foods that require much chewing

- Pay attention to the interviewer

Try to:

- Choose a food in the same price range as your interviewer

- Make sure your mouth and chin are clean after eating

When the bill arrives, the rules are simple:

- If the interviewer invited you, then the interviewer pays

- If you initiated the meeting, then you pay

THE SECOND INTERVIEW

A second interview is an excellent sign and means you are getting close to being offered a job. In some technical job interviews, a second interview is to be expected. A second interview is usually scheduled to discuss:

- Salary
- Benefits

- Employee guidelines

This second interview allows you to see the office culture, the staff, and the place where you will work. You can ask for a tour of the building while you are there.

CHAPTER 18:
AFTER THE INTERVIEW

After each interview, write notes about what went well and what went wrong. Note the problems you had and any apparent weaknesses. Even now, your work is not done. Hopefully, toward the end of the interview, you asked when a decision would be made. You need to:

- Make sure you have a business card from each person who interviewed you.

- Write thank-you notes to each interviewer after each interview, preferably within the first couple of days.

- In your note, continue to show your enthusiasm and interest in the job.

- Find out which is the best way to send the note — mail, fax, or e-mail.

- Remember to show appreciation for their consideration of you for the position.

- Make sure the note is error free.

- Do not sit and wait until you hear from them; continue to job hunt.

- Be patient.

- Follow up with a phone call within a week of sending the thank-you note.

- If you do not get the job, stay professional.

THANK-YOU NOTES

It is important to write a thank-you note right after the interview. Only hand-write the note if you have clear and legible writing. Otherwise, have someone else write the note or type it up. Keep it simple and enthusiastic.

A simple example is as follows:

Dear _____,

Thank you for the interview today. Thank you for taking the time to discuss the _____ position at _____ today. After our conversation, I am convinced that my skills and experience are an excellent fit with the position and your company.

I look forward, _____, to hearing from you regarding your hiring decision. Thank you again for your time and consideration.

Sincerely,

Your name

CHAPTER 19:
RÉSUMÉ WRITING RESOURCES

These are some wonderful resources to check out on résumés:

BOOKS

Résumés for Dummies by Joyce Lain Kennedy

The Elements of Résumé Style: Essential Rules and Eye-Opening Advice for Writing Résumés and Cover Letters That Work by Scott Bennett

Big Red Book of Résumés by McGraw Hill

Résumé Magic: Trade Secrets of a Professional Résumé Writer by S.B. Whitcomb

The Complete Idiot's Guide to the Perfect Résumé by Susan Ireland

The Damn Good Résumé Guide by Yana Parker

BROADCASTING SERVICES

- www.resumeblaster.com/dave-scripts/welcome.cfm?CODE=

CV HELP

- www.quintcareers.com/curriculum_vitae.html
- www.coloradocollege.edu/careercenter/publications/pdfs/Curriculum%20Vitae.pdf
- www.haybrook.co.uk/content_static/preparecv.asp?session_id={1DA91F98-80DE-40F2-AFCD-26273DAD4951}

EXECUTIVE JOB SEARCH INFORMATION SITES

- www.ceotrak.com

- www.executiveagent.com/career/career.html

- www.aesc.org

- www.rileyguide.com/execsrch.html#res – excellent resource for executive job search sites

GENERAL RÉSUMÉ INFORMATION

- www.cvtips.com
- www.rileyguide.com
- www.quintcareers.com

- www.careerjournal.com
- www.blueskyresumesblog.com
- www.monster.com

PORTFOLIO HELP

Portfolio Library at **http://amby.com/kimeldorf/portfolio**

RÉSUMÉ WRITING & COACHING SERVICES

Résumé Edge at **www.resumeedge.com**

Career Builder at **www.careerbuilder.com**

Jeremy Worthington at **www.buckeyeresumes.com**

Louise Fletcher at **www.blueskyresumes.com**

Janice Worthington at **www.worthingtoncareers.com**

Barbara Safani at **www.careersolvers.com**

Susan Guarneri at **www.AssessmentGoddess.com** and **www. Resume-Magic.com**

Paul Copcutt at **www.squarepegsolution.com**

Andrea Kay at **www.andreakay.com**

SECURITY INFORMATION

Pam Dixon's site at **www.pamdixon.com/index.htm**

Susan Joyce's site at **www.job-hunt.org**

VIDEO RÉSUMÉ RESOURCES

- **www.resumebook.tv**

- **www.jobmatchpro.com**

- **www.cyberviewcv.com**

CONCLUSION

If you have been following the book from start to finish, you will have learned much about yourself and the process of analyzing your skills and abilities. This, in turn, should have helped you in the process of creating a powerful résumé to help you get your next job. Like all areas of society, change is happening in the job hunting industry every day. The world is open and available like never before. You can go to a new job, a new industry, or even a new country. There is nothing stopping you.

APPENDIX A

RULES OF THE ROAD — A GUIDE TO EDITING YOUR PORTFOLIO (ART/PHOTOGRAPHY)

I. BE HONEST WITH YOURSELF.

Edit your work ruthlessly, but humanely. Ask yourself why an editor would think a particular image is interesting or powerful.

Do not assume because a bunch of people liked a particular image that it will make the cut.

If you do not know what an editor is looking for, do your homework. Find out about the newspaper, magazine, Web site, or other media and figure out what sorts of images they use. Is the publication big on sports, features, hard news? Does the publication run picture packages? Build your portfolio with a particular audience in mind. Do not assume that there is a one-size-fits-all preference to editing your work. Take editing seriously. Spend the time it takes to ask yourself some hard questions about the images you are submitting.

II. EVERY IMAGE YOU INCLUDE SHOULD SAY SOMETHING ABOUT WHO YOU ARE AND SPEAK TO YOUR STRENGTHS WITH INTEGRITY.

Your pictures should speak from your head as well as your heart. What makes your way of seeing different from the next candidate?

Edit images down because they carry specific messages you want to send to the potential employer. Edit images because they express a particular feeling, mood, moment, and concept.

Ideas are carried by moments of truth, captured by light and arranged in time and space. If your images speak to me about your relationship to the world, to light, and with people in time and space, then you are communicating honestly. Your portfolio is what you have to say for yourself.

III. UNDERSTAND THE LIMITATIONS OF AMBIGUITY IN A FRAME.

This is a tough concept to get across to students. People read and see what they want to read and see in a frame.

People have certain tolerances for ambiguity.

If the image has a moment, but there are ambiguities in the frame that distract from getting a message and feeling across, then it might not be right for the final portfolio.

Even if an image appears to be busy, it still can have a strong central story and focus. These images are usually layered with information. I think often of Sam Abell's famous "red bucket" image of cowboys roping cattle. Although there is a lot going on in the frame, there are few ambiguities about the message. In fact, the secret to this sort of image — what gives it legs — is that you can look at the frame a dozen times and still discover something interesting in it. Mary Ellen Mark, Susan Meiselas, Diane Arbus, Eugene Richards, Alex Webb, and so many others possess the skill of editing for layers of meaning in a frame.

IV. DO NOT EDIT TO THE WEAKEST FRAME.

If you do not have the best images in any specific category, why include them?

Many students think that they have it all. We think we have to have four fantastic sports action pictures, four amazing breaking and general news images, four graphically appealing features, four of this and four of that, and then a picture story to top it all off in our portfolios.

It would be ideal if a portfolio showed excellence in all these areas, but this is not always realistic. Do not overshoot your mark. Select the media that matches your ability. If you have never had an internship before, sending your work to a major daily may be problematic.

Traditionally, portfolios have been designed to show editors that a candidate can do it all: sports, news, features, and picture stories.

This may still be true to some extent, but what I think editors are really looking for today is something a bit more complex.

First and foremost, your work must show technical and compositional competence. Clear focus, ability to read and capture light, movement, and the decisive moment are givens. If you have 15 or 20 pictures in a portfolio, and only six or eight images show these competencies, what message are you sending to an editor? The message you are sending is that more than half your portfolio actually shows incompetence.

V. BE A PEOPLE PERSON.

I know that the term "people person" is on the list of 25 words not to include in your résumé, but interpersonal skills go a very long way with editors.

Being a good photographer is important, but being a good human is even more important. Take care that the images you select speak to who you are as a human being. Being a "people person" means that you demonstrate a unique insight, vision, and empathy for the people, places, and things you photograph. I think editors are looking for individuals who are going to fit in with the established culture in the newsroom.

If the editor, by looking at your pictures and reading your cover letter and résumé, gets the sense that you will not quite fit in with the culture and climate of the news organization, then your success may be limited.

VI. GET GOOD ADVICE.

Listen, look and learn from others.

If you are looking at a particular newspaper for an internship or job, why not track down someone who has been there? It is all right to have others see your work and offer opinions, but the final judgment is not yours or theirs.

Understand what you need and where you want to be.

Clarify your goals and ambitions before going to the expense of burning many CD-ROMs or printing many images. Find people that have "been there and done that" and ask them for a favor. Ask people you respect to help you edit your work.

Ask people you know who have experience with hiring interns or first-time hires. Use intelligence, common sense, and discretion in applying any advice to what you want to do in your life.

VII. EDIT FOR YOUR AUDIENCE.

Do not fool yourself into thinking you know what a good image is. Everyone has a different opinion when it comes to evaluating what a "good image" is.

Understand that there are certain conventions, standards, ideals, expectations, characteristics, and attributes good images share. Do your homework to see how your images compare with others that are winning awards and getting published.

You must understand all of these aspects and then acquire a mindset and attitude that will help you make the right choices. Your job in editing your portfolio is to communicate clearly and effectively with your audience.

The audience, in this case, is the person who wants to hire you. The audience is the person who needs you, but you have to do your part.

Do not assume that just because you send them some images that you are automatically the right fit.

If you think every image you make is "good" or that there is nothing more to learn about making images, then you could very well be missing the point. Not every image is a "good image."

However, what does seem to help in evaluating pictures is what I call the test of the (i)s: Immediacy, Intensity and Intimacy.

The three (i)s can help you to evaluate various characteristics of the images you are thinking about for your portfolio.

For example, if an image has a busy background with no clear and distinct center of impact in the frame, then it is probably lacking immediacy.

IMMEDIACY

Immediacy is the first level of the (i). Immediacy refers to the speed and comprehension in which meaning is conveyed in a frame. In typography and design we talk a lot about immediacy in terms of legibility and readability. In photography, these qualities translate to immediacy. Immediacy hooks the reader like a good lead on a news story. Immediacy suggests that there is a direction and trueness of course to the meaning of an image. Immediacy can also suggest importance and directness. Immediacy is about the expected response and the contract you have with your audience to communicate and convey a message.

INTENSITY

The second level of the (i) is intensity. Intensity refers to the qualities in an image that appeal to me emotionally and intellectually. When you have immediacy in a frame with intensity, the image appears contextual. A mug shot or real estate picture may have immediacy — we get it: this is a face; this is a house — but what it is missing is intensity. Intensity in a frame means there is a forcefulness of expression. Intensity means power and force. Your images should have power and force in order to communicate with your audience, the editor, clearly and immediately. Decisive moment images, especially in the context of sports action, usually have intensity. Nevertheless, every image in your edit must tell a story with some sort of intensity. The images, even in implicit and subtle ways, must have power, hold focus, or possess some degree of strength.

INTIMACY

Finally, there is the third level (i) of evaluating images — intimacy.

Pictures that possess immediacy and intensity usually have some impact, but what really makes images stick is intimacy. Intimacy is a feeling of closeness with what we experience in looking at a picture. It is a visual encounter that indicates a deep connection with some feeling or thoughts we have. If a picture in a portfolio has intimacy, it expresses some essential and innermost feeling and brings the viewer into it. Eugene Richards makes intimate images for me, as does Mary Ellen Mark. Larry Burrows' images from Vietnam are intimate in many ways.

I do not have a tried-and-true formula for editing, but I do know that if images have immediacy, intensity, and intimacy, they will have a good chance of standing out. Through the three (i)s, we can let our pictures speak for not only what we do, but who we are as human beings.

A word of caution about all of this. Rubrics like the three (i)s are simply ways for organizing our thoughts and images. There are many ways to be successful at picture editing and each individual must discover what works for them over time.

Reprinted by permission of Dennis Dunleavy.

APPENDIX B

Kimiko Lieberman
453 Tenth Avenue
Vancouver, British Columbia
H3V 2L1
E-mail: klieberman@xanada.com
604-373-5024 (cell)

CARER OBJECTIVE

A career in the hospitality industry that enabling me to combine my love of travel with a passion for providing outstanding customer service.

COMPETENCIES

- Dedicated to customer satisfaction

- Commitment to continuous process improvement

- Excellent presentation skills

- Excellent communication and interpersonal skills

- Experience working with diverse cultures

Languages: English, Japanese, German, French

Computer Skills: Microsoft Office (Word, Excel, PowerPoint, Outlook), Internet, Dreamweaver

ACADEMIC QUALIFICATIONS

2003   Intensive training in customer service, Carnival Cruises, Toronto

2001   Certificate in Teaching English as a Second Language, Languages International, Vancouver, British Columbia

1997   Bachelor of Commerce, University of British Columbia, Vancouver, British Columbia

PROFESIONAL EXPERIENCE

January 2005 – present, Executive Assistant to the President, Canada-Japan Cruises, Richmond, British Columbia. Responsible for:

SAMPLE RÉSUMÉS WITH CRITIQUES

- Attending meetings and writing letters on behalf of the president

- Preparing briefing notes and presentations for the president

- Liaising with directors and senior clients on behalf of the present

- Providing human resource guidance to four directors

- Supervising a staff of four administrative personnel

January 2003 – December 2004, Senior Representative, Corporate Services, Carnival Cruises, Miami, Florida. Responsible for:

- Promoting theme tours to corporate clients from Canada

- Developing marketing plans and high-end promotional packages for international corporate clients

- Analyzing trends

- Preparing budgeting projections

January 2000 – December 2002, Customer Representative, Carnival Cruises, Miami, Florida. Responsible for:

- Booking reservations on cruises

- Organizing and animating special events on cruises

- Monitoring client satisfaction and tracking client participation in special events

- Compiling and analyzing weekly quality reports for different travel destinations and making recommendations for change based on assessments

- Negotiating with travel agents and clients

- Problem solving: Anticipating and proactively resolving client concerns

- Resolving customer complaints by negotiating with the supplier on behalf of the client

May 1997 – Sept. 1999, Customer Service and Quality Control Agent, Canada–Japan Tours, Richmond, British Columbia. Responsible for:

- Staffing: Interviewed potential employees and trained junior agents

- Opened, investigated and finalized client files

- Assessed destination publications and Web site information

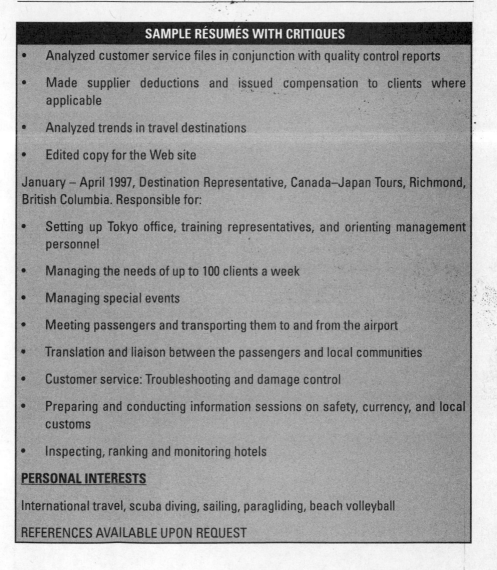

SAMPLE RÉSUMÉS WITH CRITIQUES

- Analyzed customer service files in conjunction with quality control reports

- Made supplier deductions and issued compensation to clients where applicable

- Analyzed trends in travel destinations

- Edited copy for the Web site

January – April 1997, Destination Representative, Canada–Japan Tours, Richmond, British Columbia. Responsible for:

- Setting up Tokyo office, training representatives, and orienting management personnel

- Managing the needs of up to 100 clients a week

- Managing special events

- Meeting passengers and transporting them to and from the airport

- Translation and liaison between the passengers and local communities

- Customer service: Troubleshooting and damage control

- Preparing and conducting information sessions on safety, currency, and local customs

- Inspecting, ranking and monitoring hotels

PERSONAL INTERESTS

International travel, scuba diving, sailing, paragliding, beach volleyball

REFERENCES AVAILABLE UPON REQUEST

CRITIQUE

Kimiko's résumé is solid, but has some obvious flaws that suggest it was written hastily and not proofed: "CARER OBJECTIVE," "that enabling me," and "PROFESIONAL EXPERIENCE."

Had the career objective been spelled correctly, it would have had a much greater impact on the reader because the objective is well stated and conveys the applicant's interests and the type of organization for which the applicant would like to work.

The résumé should not exceed two pages. This is the way it arrived on a recruiter's desk.

SAMPLE RÉSUMÉS WITH CRITIQUES

KIM B. KIM

321 Ash Street
Montreal, Qc J4Z IZ6
450-453-7845

Objective: Obtain a challenging position in banking or facilities management to enable me to use my facilities management and information management skills.

EMPLOYMENT

Supervisor, Flor Maintenance Systems, 2000 – present
Montreal, (Quebec)

- Oversee building operations for two office towers with 150 offices
- Responsible for supervising office-cleaning staff of six
- Schedule work and ensure compliance with labour code regulations
- Recruit, hire, train, and supervise employees
- Oversee a budget of approx. $250,000 annually
- Liaise with customers to ensure client satisfaction

CHURCH OF ST. PETER AND ST. PAUL
Montreal, QC
Facility Manager 1995 – 1999

- Responsible for upkeep & all aspects of building operations
- Manage two custodians, service, supplies, ordering, safety, first aid, fire alarm procedures & reporting activities
- Order custodial supplies for entire building
- Coordinate, schedule & supervise sub-trades & personnel
- Write performance appraisals & disciplinary letters, assist with hiring process

SAMPLE RÉSUMÉS WITH CRITIQUES

- Conduct building inspections to ensure compliance of building & safety codes, set up & maintain security alarm codes

- Write polices, procedures, job descriptions, correspondence & letters

Custodian 1997 – 1998

- Manage building & grounds, light & heavy duty custodial activities

TORONTO DOMINION BANK
Beaconsfield, Québec

Mortgage Centre
Investigation Specialist 1988 – 1995

- Researched all documentation & accounting entries pertinent to problems under investigation

- Recalculated mortgage loans, prepared entry adjustments & controlled corrective measures, confirming result & accuracy of system information

- Reported & documented system discrepancies & recommended corrective action

- Responsible for all letters to customer relations department, investigated & resolved concerns promptly to maintain a high standard of customer service

- Liaised with Mortgage Service Centers & branches across Canada to clarify procedures & resolve mortgage queries

- Supervised operations in regular supervisor's absence

MORTGAGE CENTRE
Junior Investigator 1985 – 1988

- Input journal entries and prepared cheques within discretionary limits

- Researched routine queries for mortgage and line of credit applications

- Identified transaction discrepancies between customers & bank, and brought them to the supervisor's attention

EDUCATION

ST. LAMBERT CEGEP
St. Lambert, Quebec

1984   Certificate in Financial Applications for Non-Financial Managers

SAMPLE RÉSUMÉS WITH CRITIQUES

1988   Management Training, Toronto Dominion Bank

1989   Information Management Systems, Toronto Dominion Bank

CONCORDIA UNIVERSITY
Montreal, Quebec

1995   Introduction to databases; Managing a database

1996   Introduction to C++

1997   Lotus Notes

1998   SAP

JOHN RENNIE HIGH SCHOOL
Dorval, Quebec

1984   Awarded Secondary Completion Certificate

LANGUAGES

English, French, Italian

COMPUTER SKILLS

Advanced Microsoft Office, Elementary programming, Intermediate database management

PERSONAL DATA

Single

Date of birth: October 15, 1967

Male

VOLUNTEER EXPERIENCE

Habitat for Humanity

March of Dimes

REFERENCES AVAILABLE ON REQUEST

CRITIQUE

Here we have inconsistent use of heading sizes, formats, and positioning:

KIM B. KING is written in upper case — all right, but the address seems isolated on the far right of page; it would look better left-aligned.

"Supervisor, Flor Maintenance Systems" is written in lower case, but "CHURCH OF ST. PETER AND ST. PAUL" is not.

Inconsistent spelling of Quebec in full and abbreviated: Montreal, (Quebec), Qc, QC, Québec.

PERSONAL DATA – should not be included on a résumé.

SAMPLE RÉSUMÉS WITH CRITIQUES

Rose Alexandra Bergin
3574 MacDonald Avenue
Montreal, Quebec H4V 1H2
Telephone: (514) 332-2698 (cell)
E-mail: colourmepinklips@yahoo.com

CAREER OBJECTIVE: To pursue a career in film or animation and produce videos or films that are entertaining yet socially and culturally relevant.

SUMMARY OF QUALIFICATIONS

Five years of communications experience (management of a Web site, production of a promotional video, brochures, magazines, newsletters, special-events planning, editing of a short animated feature)

Highly developed interpersonal skills

Extremely creative

Thrive under pressure

Very strong computer skills (InDesign, Photoshop, Dreamweaver)

Bilingual (English and French)

EMPLOYMENT EXPERIENCE

2004 – present   Editor, Luxor Productions, Montreal

Responsible for producing print and video communications, including a monthly electronic bulletin, a flagship corporate production, as well as an award-winning video promoting the organization to its clients.

SAMPLE RÉSUMÉS WITH CRITIQUES

Promotional video shortlisted for regional competition

Organized photo shoots for print and Web use

Prepared style guides for writers and photographers

2002 – 2004   Junior Editor, Miss Quebec, Montreal

Input and proofed copy for one of Quebec's top teen magazines

Wrote fashion copy and attended fashion shows and unveilings by Quebec designers

EDUCATION

1998 – 2001, School of Fine Arts, Concordia University, Montreal

Graduated with an Honours degree in Fine Arts, specializing in film production

1996 – 1998, Web Design, LaSalle College, Montreal

Graduated with a diploma in Web design and animation

COMMUNITY EXPERIENCE

Wrote, edited, and produced a short video for AIDS awareness campaign aimed at university students

Contributed to the organization of a charity fashion auction that raised $10,000 for cancer research

CRITIQUE

This is a very clean-looking résumé, neatly spaced, with consistent headings and use of type faces. The author's selective use of color suggests a creative aspect to her personality. The only drawback to this résumé is the author's e-mail address. "Colourmepinklips" could lead to a recruiter not taking the applicant seriously, despite the applicant's otherwise stellar résumé. The applicant could change the name to "colour me pink" which is catchy, and could reflect a brand.

DEDICATION/BIOGRAPHY

This book is dedicated to my loving circle of family and friends, who may have raised a questioning eyebrow at the various paths I have chosen in life, but have never let that stop them from supporting me along the way.

Dale Mayer is a certified technical writer, editor, and researcher with a passion for the written word. For over a decade, she has honored that passion both at work and at home. Besides her very busy freelance business, she is also an avid writer of fiction. At this time, she has completed five novels; her sixth is in progress with an additional five completed screenplays to her credit. She enjoys writing nonfiction as it forces her brain out of the clouds and back to the world in which we all live. Dale finds researching, writing, and organizing all the parts and pieces together into a coherent and easy-to-read package to be just plain fun! She can be contacted through her Web site, **www.dalemayer.com**.

GLOSSARY

Accomplishments — These are the highlights of your career; the achievements from your work history that will help to prove your candidacy to a potential employer. You focus your cover letters, résumés, and even job interviews on these accomplishments.

Action Verbs — These are descriptive verbs that effectively express your skill set, accomplishments, and experience. Start each sentence with an action verb. Try to avoid using any forms of the verb "to be." Also, avoid using nondescriptive verbs.

Assessment Tests — These tests ask questions in an effort to provide insight into a person's personality and potential careers for them. These tests do not give a complete picture; however, they are a good place to start if you are considering what might be the best careers for you.

Background Check — A check done by employers to confirm the information you provided on your résumé. This check can include employment information, education, references, credit, medical records, criminal record, and more.

Behavioral Interview — An interview style where behavioral questions are asked.

Behavioral Questions — Questions that

an interviewer will ask such as examples of a time when you had to do something specific. This technique is used to see how fast you can react, how quickly you think on your feet, and how well you can pull from your experience to handle critical issues.

Benefits — An important part of your hiring package and part of the salary negotiation process. Benefits can include paid vacations, personal days, sick days, life insurance, medical insurance, tuition, personal development, childcare assistance, stock options, and even pension plans.

Branding — See Career Branding.

Career Assessment — See Assessment Tests.

Career Branding — This is how you define who you are, how you are perceived, and why people should seek you. Branding is your reputation — how you build your name. It is what identifies you and shows the added value you bring to an employer.

Career Change — This is when you change from one career, where the bulk of your experience lies, to another career. In today's economic situation, the average person will change careers three to five times in a lifetime.

Career Coach — A professional who specializes in helping people make career and life management decisions. They are also called career consultants, career advisors, work-life coaches, and personal career trainers.

Career Exploration — This is the process of exploring career choices, various paths, and specific jobs to find a more rewarding career.

Career Fair — Where a company puts on an event to bring in potential job candidates while giving these candidates a chance to learn more about the company.

Career Objective — This is an optional section at the top of your résumé. It should reflect how you can benefit the employer.

Career Portfolio — See Job Skills Portfolio.

Career Research — See Career Exploration.

Career Planning — This is the ongoing evaluation process of your career to date, making adjustments and then improvements to create the career you want.

Career Vision Statement — The long-term career goals of a job seeker. This statement gives a clear direction for the future.

Chronological Résumé — A résumé organized by your employment history in reverse chronological order.

Cold Call — A job hunter contacts a potential employer who has no known job openings.

Compensation Package — This is the combined salary and benefits offered by a company.

Contract Employee — Where you work for one organization (and its salary and benefit structure) that sells your services to another company on a project or time basis. Compare to Freelancer.

Corporate Culture — This term is the collection of beliefs and values shared by an organization's members. The culture sets the rules of conduct, which define what is acceptable behavior for the employees. This culture is important to understand to see if you will fit in and enjoy being there before accepting a job.

Counter Offer — This a technique used by a job seeker in response to an unacceptable job offer. This counter offer is looking to change one of the negotiable elements of a job and can include salary, nonsalary compensation, moving expenses, benefits, and any other job-specific issues.

Cover Letter — This letter should always accompany your résumé when you apply for a position. It should interest a recruiter or hiring manager in reading your résumé.

Curriculum Vitae (CV) — This is a written description of your work experience, education, and skills. It is more detailed than a résumé. It is common in other parts of the world and is the norm for someone in the academic world.

Declining Letter — This letter is sent to a company when a person is turning down a job offer. Make sure to be polite and professional.

Degree — This is a level of education achieved in an academic setting from a unified program of study.

Electronic Résumé — A résumé that will be sent to the employer electronically, via e-mail, or by either submitting to Internet job boards or one residing on the company's Web page.

E-mail Cover Letter — An e-mail cover letter accompanies a résumé that is sent to the employer electronically via e-mail. See also Cover Letter.

Employment Gaps — The periods of time when a job hunter was unemployed. These gaps should be minimized and will need to be explained.

Employment Testing — Tests that job candidates may be asked to take. Tests can include aptitude, skills, literacy, personality, medical, and drug tests.

Exit Interview — A meeting between an employee who has resigned or been terminated and the company.

Freelancer/Consultant/Independent Contractor — This term applies to people who work for themselves and put in bids for projects with different companies. This can still be a full-time job and allows freedom, flexibility, and job satisfaction.

Group Interview — See Panel Interview.

Functional Résumé — A résumé organized by skills and functions.

Hidden Job Market — This is the market of jobs that are never publicly known and can be very difficult to hear about without digging, either through networking or cold calling. See Networking and Cold Call.

Home-Based Career — A career based on working from the home.

Informational Interview — An interview where you go speak to someone, looking for information from them. This information can be for many different reasons, but it is most often used to learn about different careers. You would speak to someone who is working in a career you are interested in so you can ask him or her about it.

Internship — This involves working in your field either during school or over the summer. It is a good way to gain work experience, especially for entry-level job hunters.

Interview — See Job Interview.

Job Objective — See Career Objective.

Job Application — A paper form that requires you to fill out many questions. It is often a duplicate of your résumé, but still needs to be filled out carefully, honestly, and clearly.

Job Board — These are sometimes called job sites. There are several different types of job boards like general, industry specific, geographic, niche specific, and company centers.

Job Fair — See Career Fair.

Job Interview — A meeting between a job candidate and an interviewer looking to hire the right person. Questions are asked about experience, accomplishments, and skills to determine whether they are a good match.

Job Satisfaction — A term to describe how happy a person is with their job. It takes into consideration the work, compensation, and whether the person feels valued, among other things.

Job Shadowing — Provides a job hunter an opportunity to go to the place of work of a person doing a job that the job hunter is considering. This allows the job hunter to "shadow" the person and gain valuable inside information as to what the job is like.

Job Skills — These are the required skills to complete a specific job. In any industry, whether it be medical, legal or even construction, a specific set of skills are required to complete the job with any level of competence.

Job Skills Portfolio — A portfolio is a collection of your work that highlights your accomplishments.

Key Accomplishments — Also called Qualifications Summary, this is a section in your résumé that summarizes (using nouns as keywords and descriptors) your major career accomplishments.

Keywords — This term refers to single words or phrases that highlight your skills. The keywords are usually specific to your profession and would be easily recognized by any potential recruiter or employer. Job titles, certificates held as well as technological terms could be included as keywords.

Letter of Acceptance — This letter is the formal acceptance you send back to a potential employer when you accept their job offer. Included in this letter should be the offer, the date you agree to start as well as a full listing of all the conditions that have been agreed on.

Letter of Recommendation — A letter written to support your skills, ability, and work ethic, usually written when applying to graduate school.

Mentor — A person who counsels, advises, and helps guide you. This type of relationship will have an impact on your personal growth, career development, goal achievement, and other areas mutually designated by the mentor and partner.

Moonlighting — Refers to the practice of working at multiple jobs.

Networking — Contacting others through social, professional, and business functions. These people can help you to find job leads, offer advice and information about a particular company, and introduce you to other people, thus increasing your network.

Nontraditional Careers — Careers where less than 25 percent of the workforce is of one gender.

Occupational Outlook Handbook — Published by the U.S. Department of Labor, Bureau of Labor Statistics, this guide provides detailed information on more than 250 occupations. The *Handbook* discusses the nature of the work and the typical working conditions for persons in each occupation. In addition, it details the requirements for entry and the opportunities for advancement.

Offer of Employment — An offer to a job seeker, which specifies the term of the arrangement, including the start date, salary, and benefits.

Older Workers — Job hunters older than 45 years.

Online Recruitment — Uses the Internet to advertise job vacancies and to manage applications. This system streamlines the recruitment process.

Overqualified — A problem of people who appear to have too much experience and education, and were too highly paid in previous positions.

Panel/Group Interviews — An interview conducted by a committee of people asking questions.

Passive Job Search — When you are not openly searching for a new job but are keeping an interest in new possibilities by continuing to network.

Personal Mission Statement — How a job hunter identifies his or her values and beliefs. It offers a chance to establish what is important.

Phone Interview — A job interview that is conducted via telephone.

Qualifications Summary — See Key Accomplishments.

Recruiters — Professionals who find candidates for specific positions.

Referral Letter — A type of cover letter that uses name dropping to attract the reader and get an interview.

Reference List — The list of people whom a prospective employer can contact for references.

References — People who know you and will say good things about you. They could be coworkers, educational references, or even personal references.

Researching Companies — Gathering information about a certain company, including its products, locations, and successes.

Resignation — When you decide it is time to leave your job, you do it in writing as your official resignation.

Résumé — A key job hunting tool used to get an interview, it summarizes your accomplishments, education, and work experience, and should reflect your special mix of skills and strengths.

Salary — The money you will receive for doing a certain job. This can include overtime pay, bonuses, and commissions.

Salary History — A prospective employer may request that you send them a history of the salaries you have received in your previous jobs. Include the amount of the full compensation package and not just the salary.

Salary Negotiation — The process of obtaining the best compensation package possible.

Salary Requirements — This is the salary you require to take a job that a company is considering offering you.

Scannable Résumé — A résumé that has been prepared to be scanned into a company's database.

Screening Interview — A meeting designed to weed out unqualified candidates. It is important to provide the facts about your skills rather than just establishing rapport.

Telecommuting — When a person works from another location, usually home, for one or more days in a week.

Temping — The situation where a person works for a limited time with a company that needs temporary help.

Temporary (Temp) Agency — A company that places personnel in jobs on a short-term or contract basis.

Text Résumé — Also referred to as text-based or ASCII résumé, a résumé that has been optimized for an electronic résumé database or electronic résumé tracking system.

Thank-You Letter — After every interview, you should send a thank-you letter to each person who interviewed you.

Traditional Interview — In this type of interview, you will be asked basic questions like, "Why do you want to work for this company?" and "Why are you the best person for this position?"

Transferable Skills — Skills you have acquired from any part of your life that are transferable to your next job.

Underqualified — This is when you do not have the required qualifications for a position.

Video Résumé — A résumé created in video format.

Web-Based Résumé — A résumé that is on the Internet.

Workplace Values — The concepts and ideas that define how a job seeker looks at his or her job.

BIBLIOGRAPHY

BOOKS

Bennett, Scott. (2005). *The Elements of Résumé Style: Essential Rules and Eye-Opening Advice for Writing Résumés and Cover Letters That Work*. New York: AMACOM – American Management Association

McGraw-Hill's Big Red Book of Résumés, (2002). Chicago: McGraw Hill.

Kennedy, Joyce Lain. (2007). *Résumés for Dummies* (4th ed.). New York: Wiley Publishing.

Whitcomb, S. B. (2007). *Résumé Magic: Trade Secrets of a Professional Résumé Writer* (3rd ed.). Indianapolis, IN: JIST Publishing.

Whitcomb, S. B. (2003). *Résumé Magic: Trade Secrets of a Professional Résumé Writer* (2nd ed.). Indianapolis, IN: JIST Publishing.

INTERNET

About.com — Job Search Center

   http://jobsearch.about.com

About.com — Desktop Publishing

   http://desktoppub.about.com/ od/e-mailclasses/a/1portfolio_ why_2.htm

   http://desktoppub.about.com/cs/ freelance/a/portfolio_2.htm

About.com — Career Planning Center

   http://careerplanning.about. com/od/jobsearch/a/Internet_ search.htm

The Career Journal

   http://www.careerjournal.com

Network Services & Consulting Corporation

   http://www.enetsc.com

AARP — American Association of Retired Persons

   http://www.aarp.org/money/ careers/findingajob/resumes/ a2004-05-28-rightresume.html

Chili Jobs Web Site

   http://www.chilijobs.com/ resumewriting/center_4j.asp

Writing Help Central

http://www.writinghelp-central.com/article-recommendation-letter.html

Job Web — For New Graduates

http://www.jobweb.com

Women for Hire

http://www.womenforhire.com/advice/resumes_examples_and_cover_letter_templates/chronological_resume_template

Saskatchewan Government Web Site

http://www.sasked.gov.sk.ca/docs/midcareer/appendc.html

Job Street

http://sg.jobstreet.com/career/writing/resume4.htm

Jumpstart Your Job Search Web Site

http://www.jumpstartyourjob-search.com

College Graduate Web Site

http://www.collegegrad.com

Monster Job Search Web Site

http://content.monster.com/articles/3475/17204/1/home.aspx

http://content.monster.com/articles/3477/18577/1/home.aspx

Résumé Power — Criminal Record Article

http://www.resumepower.com/criminal-record-resume.html

Distinctive Documents

http://www.distinctiveweb.com

Suite101.com

http://selfemployment.suite101.com/blog.cfm/how_to_self_evaluate

Résumé Resource

http://www.resume-resource.com/article30.html

Military Résumé Wizard

www.militaryresumewizard.com

The Riley Guide

www.rileyguide.com

Ezine Articles

http://ezinearticles.com/?Being-Overqualified-For-A-Job-Is-No-Longer-A-Stigma&id=85311

AOL — Find a Job

http://jobs.aol.com/article/_a/overqualified-for-the-job-six-interview/20050808184809990006

Quintessential Careers

http://www.quintcareers.com/
underqualified-unqualified_
job-seeker.html

Job Bank USA

http://www.jobbankusa.
com/CareerArticles/Resume/
ca111506h.html

Student Résumé Help

http://www.bishopblanchet.
org/files/counseling/sturesume.
pdf

Teach Net Web Site

http://www.teachnet.com/
how-to/employment/portfolios/
port004.html

Ball State University — Career Center

http://www.bsu.edu/students/
careers/media/pdf/portfoli.pdf

http://www.bsu.edu/students/
careers/article/0,1370,192168-2
194-32707,00.html

What Is a Design—Tech Portfolio?

http://books.elsevier.
com/bookscat/
samples/9780240807126/
Sample_Chapters/02-chapter_
one.pdf

Art-Support

http://www.art-support.com/
portfolio.htm

Ryerson University — Portfolio Writing

http://www.ryerson.ca/career/
tools/portfolio_writing.
html#2_3

CV Tips

http://www.cvtips.com/one_to_
one_job_interview.html

Centennial College

www.centennialcollege.ca

Flying Solo — Article on Personal
Branding Strategies

http://www.flyingsolo.com.au

Career Board

http://www.careerboard.com/
janice/job-search-tips.html

Dennis Dunleavy

http://ddunleavy.typepad.com/
the_big_picture

http://www.technorati.com/
people/technorati/ddunleavy

Mary Anne Thompson Web Site

http://www.goinglobal.com

Jeremy Worthington Web Site

  http://www.buckeyeresumes.com

Blue Sky Résumés

  http://www.blueskyresumes.com

  http://www.blueskyresumesblog.com

Janice Worthington

  http://www.worthingtoncareers.com

Barbara Safani

  http://www.careersolvers.com

Susan Guarneri

  http://www.AssessmentGoddess.com

  http://www.Resume-Magic.com

Paul Copcutt

  http://www.squarepegsolution.com

Andrea Kay

  http://www.andreakay.com

Martin Kimeldorf

  http://amby.com/kimeldorf/portfolio

INDEX